How to Talk to Spirits

Séances • Mediums • Ghost Hunts

JUNE AHERN

ISBN: 1542641292
ISBN 13: 9781542641296

Cover: Jeremy Taylor. www.jeremytaylor.eu
Author Photograph: Jerry Briesach

Books By June Ahern

Parapsychology, Metaphysical
The Timeless Counselor: The Best Guide to a Successful Psychic Reading

Novels:
The Skye in June
City of Redemption

SPECIAL DEDICATION

*To Chad Ramirez and the many curious living that inspired
sharing my ghostly experiences.*

■ ■ ■

TABLE OF CONTENTS

HOW IT BEGAN

From ghoulies and ghostie
And long-leggedy beasties
And things that go bump in the night,
Good Lord, deliver us!

— Scottish Poem, Anonymous —

Why do I believe in ghosts, spirits and life after death? I've experienced all three. For over forty years I worked as a psychic medium, metaphysical and occult teacher as well as been active as a student of parapsychology and psychic phenomena. I retired from my practice in 2013, but my interest and studies continue. I had no intention of writing a book about this subject even though asked many times to do so. Finally, after a constant plea from some former clients I agreed to write it with the purpose of addressing questions asked of me as well as what I have taught about communicating with spirits. I have continued to receive questions from the curious living (see questions in Chapter 1) and have learned more through my ghost investigations as well as personal spirit communications thus a second edition was necessary.

Personally and professionally I have encountered, experienced and learned about out-of-body and paranormal experiences. This book contains many of my own experiences and those of others as well as questions from people interested in spirit communication and curious about ghost sightings. In it you will learn about the phenomena of spirit and ghost manifestations and communication. You will discover ways of making contact with spirits when alone or in a crowded room, through dreams, séances, or during psychic readings. You are encouraged to experiment and allow your experiences to reveal whether talking to the dead is a reality or even a possibility. If you follow my suggestions for communicating with your loved ones after death, I sincerely hope you find the answers and comfort you seek.

In 1970, after a serious automobile accident and while in the ambulance, I expired for a moment and was subsequently revived. This was my first experience with a spirit connection. For many years after this incident, I couldn't talk about my profound experience of being on the other side. How could I explain that I saw *the light*? How could I describe the ecstatic sense of pure joy and serenity unknown to me previously in this life?

Outside the crashed vehicle, a white light appeared to emanate from a woman standing close by. She stared at me intently through the windshield as I sat bleeding profusely from head and face injuries. Dazed, I looked back at her. Her presence was comforting and her face kind. Surrounded by a glow of light, she appeared to be clothed in all white. I felt loving warmth from the woman and thought I heard her say, "Don't worry, it'll be alright." But that was impossible given the distance between us. Then the light enveloped me. Only I wasn't led through a tunnel as others who have died and returned say they experienced. The next thing I recall was a policeman sitting in the driver's seat next to me telling me to hang on. I knew he was talking to me but I couldn't focus on him. All I could think about as blood poured onto my new coat was how my clothes were ruined. It's strange what bothers us in serious situations. I don't recall being carried from the wreck to the ambulance or even the ride to the hospital.

With time, I remembered my journey to the other side. Once you have come back from the brink of death, you're never quite the same. What happened during that time, how you felt, what you saw always remains vivid in your mind. I saw deceased relatives, some gone for many years. Some I only recognized because of old photographs in family albums. In a beautiful garden, they were laughing softly, their faces full of peace and love. A warm bright light surrounded the whole scene. An ornate white iron fence encircled the garden. I stood outside the fence, gazing at my happy grandparents, uncles and aunts. They watched me with big smiles. I felt peace and heartfelt love. Then they began to wave me away, cheerily saying, "Not now, June. Go back."

The next thing I saw were bright lights moving rapidly above me as I was wheeled into the emergency ward. Many hands probed, and voices asked too many questions. My clothes were cut off and needles pierced my face. It felt raw, and the pain was excruciating. Survival took over and recovery took a long time. While I was in the hospital, the police officer visited for information about the driver. Was he sober? On drugs? The driver, as it turns out, was under the influence of drugs and fell asleep at the wheel. We hit a utility pole head-on with no seat belts. This was before seat belts were common, or the law. I was ejected through the windshield. Then as I reentered the vehicle, jagged glass ripped and embedded into my face. The policeman told me a young couple saw the crash but didn't leave their car after flagging down help. There was no one else at the scene. My woman in white wasn't a witness. She didn't exist according to the policeman. Later, my surgeon told me I was a lucky young woman because I expired in the ambulance for about twenty seconds. Twenty seconds that changed my life forever.

My near-death experience (NDE) was pushed into the background as I struggled through a very lengthy recovery. My life was forever altered, not only physically and emotionally, but also spiritually. Not only did the accident leave me with serious facial scars, but also psychic abilities to see and hear spirits of the dead and identify things about people without ever having met them before. I had to accept these abilities would transform my life forever.

It was frightening and confusing for a nineteen-year-old woman to see, hear and know facts about living and dead people. I fretted and wondered about these strange happenings. NDE, at this time, was rarely, if ever, discussed. People dismissed individuals such as myself with NDE experiences as delusional, fakes or odd. It was also a huge time of change both socially and politically. This may be why, in time, I gave to the fact my outlook on life was different. I could hear, see, feel, and even smell non-physical people as though if they were in front of me. And with acceptance came the desire to know more about it.

Had I really been on the other side? Was it a miracle I came back? An opportunity for a second chance in life to do something meaningful I had not considered before? Seeking information and education, I talked to numerous people who might have had, or knew someone with a NDE and perhaps like me saw and heard things which physically didn't exist.

Fortunately, since then, books such as Dr. Raymond Moody Jr.'s 1975 best-seller, *Life After Life*, and more recently Anita Moorjani's 2011 *Dying To Be Me: My Journey From Cancer to Near Death, To True Healing* validate and afford a kinder response to those who have experienced NDE. Reading Dr. Moody's many case studies calmed my anxiety. I learned there were many individuals worldwide, and throughout history with similar experiences to mine.

If you, or someone you know, has had a NDE and wishes to understand how, why and what now or, are interested in learning more about this kind of experience, IANDS (International Association For Near Death Studies, Inc) is a good source. Know you are not alone in your experience or thoughts about this phenomenon.

A survey in *US News & World Report* of March 1997 reported 15 million people have experienced NDE. The recent most famous case is the near-death experience of ABC anchor, Bob Woodruff, who almost died from a roadside bomb explosion in Iraq. About his experience Mr. Woodruff said, "I don't remember hearing it. I remember that I——I went out for a minute. I saw my body floating below me and [a] kind of whiteness. I don't have much more information than that, whether it was heaven or something. I still don't know." [*sic*]

Elisabeth Kübler-Ross, M.D. and a psychiatrist who was a pioneer in near-death studies and the author of the groundbreaking book, *On Death and Dying* said this about death, "For those who seek to understand it, death is a highly creative force. The highest spiritual values of life can originate from the thought and study of death."

All in all, my paranormal, psychic experiences have taken me on a wonderful spiritual journey. At times the voyage has been sad and scary, but the encounters of realities beyond the physical world have brought a greater sense of self-awareness about life and the hereafter.

Did I become a different person with a greater focus than before of what my life purpose was to be? No, I didn't have any big "light bulb" moment to answer, "Why am I here?" At first I was just trying to survive and adjust to my physical injuries and the kind of changes growing up a young adult experiences. The psychic visions became of great interest and stirred me into figuring out why I had this ability and what to do with it.

My near-death experience gave me the chance to meet so many people from all over the United States, as well as diverse parts of the world. The psychic readings I gave them made me aware that numerous people from every walk of life and culture are interested in metaphysical and paranormal occurrences.

It truly has been a gift to me. I've shared this gift with many people teaching them to be more aware of and to increase their own psychic abilities. When people question my psychic abilities, I explain, "When a computer's hard drive is wiped clean it takes a special person like a computer technician to access information others cannot." I am that special person who accesses unseen information.

A good approach to understanding a subject you are unfamiliar with or suspicious of being fakery is to keep an open mind. Dr. Carl Jung, in his 1919 address to the Society for Psychical Research in England, said, "I shall not commit the fashionable stupidity of regarding everything I cannot explain as a fraud."

In this book, you will learn the proper preparation for spirit communication and interaction, whether that will be on your own, with a medium, or in a group (séance). It will teach you such things as how to set a special time to communicate with spirit energy, how to avoid attracting negative, low-grade forces, and how to deal with ghost energy. If your interest is to ghost hunt, you will be advised how to set-up a successful investigation. Your own participation in and approach to spirit communication will be influenced by your personal beliefs about death and what, if anything, happens after death. I advise you that at some point, you must end the communication to allow the spirits to continue their spiritual advancement as you continue your own advancement on Earth. Although I will suggest a time you should discontinue or limit communication with the spirits of your loved ones, you will come to recognize the right moment to do so through knowledge and experience. I have included spirit communication with pets because many of us animal lovers grieve when our pets cross over and wish to know if they are okay.

On her television show Sonya Fitzpatrick, animal psychic and author of numerous pet advice books, discussed with medium John Edwards, pet spirit communication. She read one of John's pets. John wondered why people don't believe this can be possible. Ms. Fitzpatrick answered "If one hasn't experienced it for oneself, it's difficult to believe."

Her answer seems reasonable. Once it happens, you'll believe an existence in some kind of form continues after death, even if you can't explain it. Until then it's up to you to decide whether life continues after death.

Whether you believe in Heaven or Nirvana or not, do you want to explore the possibilities of the dead existing outside the physical body? Perhaps you will succeed in realizing a heaven exists, perhaps not. Maybe you can come to a place of peace within by having your questions answered or curiosity satisfied. You may find your grief abates after spirit communication occurs. You may also change your mind about life and death. All you need to do is keep an open mind and heart. After reading the book and maybe doing what is offered to communicate with spirits, you can decide if communicating with spirits is realistic and indeed can bring comfort to the living.

In the following chapter, you will find answers to questions about spirits and ghost encounters, which might answer your curiosity about this subject.

■ ■ ■

1

QUESTIONS FROM THE CURIOUS LIVING

*The boundaries, which divide Life from Death
are at best shadowy and vague. Who shall say
where the one ends, and where the other begins?*

– Edgar Allan Poe –

People are curious about and perplexed by what happens after death, or if anything does happen at all. They wonder what the spirits of the dead might appear as, how they will manifest and what kind of messages will they give. They want to know why the spirits communicate, and if the spirits or ghosts should be feared.

For centuries people from many different cultures, countries, and religions shared stories about ghosts and their sightings. The concept of ghosts, as hopeful evidence of life after death, goes all the way back to ancient Egypt. Then it was commonly believed death was merely a transition to some mysterious netherworld of existence. In the first century A.D. during the Roman Empire period, the great Roman author and statesman Pliny the Younger recorded one of the first notable ghost stories in letters. He reported the "specter" [ghost] of an old man with a long beard, rattling chains, haunted his house in Athens. There are many ghost stories about England's Anne Boleyn, the second wife of King Henry VIII, haunting the Tower of London to sightings of Benjamin Franklin's ghost seen near the library of the American Philosophical Society in Philadelphia.

Even though many people over the course of history have experienced what they believe to be spirit communication and ghost sightings, and for some, visits from negative entities, to date there is no solid scientific proof any of this happens. Still people from all walks of life and throughout the world believe in paranormal phenomenon. There are certainly plenty of skeptics too. I am a "show me" kind of person also. I support a healthy skepticism while investigating the possibilities of paranormal phenomenon. With that attitude you take charge of an investigation. On a 2016 Dr. Oz television show, he professed he was a skeptic of spirit communication. He then introduced his guests: psychic mediums and authors, John Edwards and Char Margolis. They demonstrated their abilities by connecting some audience members to their dead relatives. One woman clearly stated before the show began and when it was on air she didn't believe it was possible to communicate with spirits. The woman then received a reading by Ms. Margolis. Imagine her surprise when she received an accurate message from beyond. Some might claim the woman was a "plant" secured by the mediums or producers to feign skepticism and then astonishment at the reading's accuracy. Others might say the medium was too vague. Some might follow the mediums with blind faith. Ultimately, only you can decide what feels valid to you.

Because of my many years of paranormal and psychic experiences, I am constantly asked for my thoughts on the subject. *Do ghosts really exist? How do I know if I've encountered one? Can I talk to the dead? Are ghosts evil?* Such curiosity is not uncommon. What most people want to know about is my experiences with the supernatural.

With my readers' interests being most important to me, I decided to place the Q&A chapter at the beginning of the book when it is normally found at the end. One or more questions might validate your personal experience with a spirit or ghost and address your burning curiosity about the paranormal.

A few months before starting this book, I sent a request to clients, former students, and friends for questions they had about psychic phenomenon. In time, others who had heard about the survey sent me their questions. I answered each to the best of my knowledge and experiences. You will notice some of the answers seem to repeat themselves. This is because, although some are similar, they could be addressed with slightly different answers.

If you would rather learn how to begin spirit communication now and come back later to the Q&A chapter, please go directly to Chapter 5.

Let's get started...

• *I've heard you talk about spirits and ghosts. Is there a difference?* To me there is a difference. Although a ghost is the spirit or energy of a person, it has not gone onto a place of peaceful rest. The entity is suspended in a limbo state——not moving onto a heaven, or another dimension or living a physical life on Earth. Long after it has left the physical body it lingers on Earth reliving the same painful, misery and/or death scene over and over again. With that said about the belief of stuck ghosts, I'll add a friendly encounter of one who had no plans to move on.

In two ghost investigations of San Francisco's infamous Barbary Coast site with The Haunted Bay, San Francisco (see Youtube.com, The Haunted Bay: Ep 3) - The Condor Club) I encountered a couple of rather cheery ghost fellows who had no plans to move on to the next dimension (the light/heaven) for the time being. My first encounter was at the well-known Condor nightclub on San Francisco's Broadway Street. I saw a big, I mean big man sitting at the end of the bar drinking a cocktail. Later, I learned it was Jimmy "The Bear" Ferrozzo, assistant manager who died in 1983 in an utterly bizarre accident at the club. Jimmy was indeed a large man and at one time tried out for the Dallas Cowboys football team. His death was accidently triggered by his foot, which killed him and injured his naked mistress beneath him. Victim to an avoidable death, he wasn't bemoaning his ghostly predicament, but rather he put it behind.

My other happy ghost was found in an alleyway. He had no mean-spirited attitude toward the living and happily greeted those who could "see" him. He told me he was a watchman at one time and continues to keep that position. When I asked him why he wasn't moving on to the light or eternal rest, he replied with a chuckle, why should he? He was quite happy where he sat giving directions and history about the area "back in the day." I think of him as a resident ghost historian. Learn more about him on Youtube.com video, The Haunted Bay-SF Barbary Coast (Ep 5) Walk with a Medium (see 6:38 minutes into the video.)

Most ghostly manifestations are not as happy with their lot in life. Ghost manifestations or appearances are often seen as disembodied person spirits. The majority of times ghosts experienced a sudden, and often tragic, violent death. For example, if a person committed suicide by hanging, you might see only the face of that person with a rope tied around the neck. Some ghosts were perpetrators of a crime. Often, the ghost was a victim who did not receive justice. It cries out for justice! Who is listening? Let's personalize the concept.

You have a situation where you felt unjustly treated, victimized or misunderstood and you play it over and over in your mind. Maybe a one-time event that hurt or shocked you. Months or years later you recall clearly what was done and said. Maybe you still talk about it as though it was yesterday the situation happened instead of some time ago. This memory is stuck in your mind, emotions and body and repeats itself as if it was happening again. You can't seem to let it go, bring it to a peaceful or sensible understanding. You may even say something like, "I'll never get over this." Well, evidently neither did the ghost. If you really want you can be reprieved from the pain of it, at least to some degree if not entirely. You can undergo therapy to help release the sorrow or anger. The ghosts also can be reprieved from their pains and anguish through your prayers and good tidings for peace. If you find the ghost hunting continues, call in a medium educated and skilled in this area to help the ghost move on.

About spirit energy: Spirit is our true self, the energy of who we are outside and inside the physical body. We can look at it as that which makes up our individual self, our character and personality. At the time of death when we take the last breath the physical body ceases to house the spirit. Some people have reported that at the time when witnessing a death they saw a light cloud or white orb (more on that later) floating up and out of the body. When I was alone with an elderly friend who died I felt, rather than saw, her energy leave her body and float up the ceiling. In panic of what to do, I called my sister. Who should I contact? What am I to do for Barbara (my dead friend)? My sister advised me to first open a window to let my friend's spirit out so she could continue her journey to the next dimension (or heaven.) The advice felt right and good so when my sister died I opened a window and wished her a speedy and blessed journey.

Spirits can, and do, come back to visit for a period of time. This period can last from one and up to four or five earthly years while adjustments are made around the separation. After a while, the spirit becomes less involved with worldly matters and relationships and communication is less frequent. There comes a time the spirit must truly rest in peace and not be called back to comfort the living. Read more about this subject in upcoming chapters and also in some questions below.

• *Do ghosts know they are ghosts?* They do. Since the majority seeks relief from their soul's pain help them separate from this world and get onto the next. If you are aware of a ghost or an unhappy spirit, prayers and good thoughts can help them rest in peace and be finished with the world. Perhaps the spirits/ghosts knowing they are seen and heard, and their pains and misfortunes understood, will decide it's time to move from the physical world to a more peaceful dimension. Unfortunately, some truly are lost souls and destined to keep repeating the same life scenarios throughout the ages. We really don't know everything about ghostly reasoning, karma and manifestations. If they become disturbing to your peace and well being you'll have to take stronger measures to rid your environment of them. Again, we'll discuss how to do that in upcoming questions and chapters.

• *Do ghost and spirits look alike?* Not to me, or others who have seen both. It's more unnerving, and sometimes frightening to actually *see* with the physical eye ghosts or spirits appear before you rather than mentally envisioning or sense them. Usually, communication with spirits and ghosts happens in the mind with worded messages and/or an image, like a face. It's a much more pleasant experience than having them physically appear in front of you.

A manifestation of a dead person is a shock to logic and reason. Still, it happens. When I experience what I deem as a physical manifestation of a spirit or ghost, I gather my wits quickly so as not to fear seeing what should not be there—logically that is.

Ghosts appear in whole form or in parts. People have told me of seeing just a hand on a doorknob or a menacing face staring through a window or a body falling down a staircase. As I said before, they are stuck in time and space and the aspects of their deaths. They can be a floating white wisp of a cloud or a bolt of energy shooting along a darkened corridor. Since ghosts aren't able or willing to disconnect from the physical plane they appear to more people than spirits do.

Spirits, unlike my ghostly encounters, come for a short time, deliver their message then fade away. Most are not much interested in staying around this world for long after leaving it. Sometime soon after leaving the physical body their physical energy begins to weaken and in time, fades away. I have learned in the spirit world, form is not easily manifested and it's rare spirits show up in a physical form. If the surge of energy isn't strong, their attempts to form are like a weak electrical current where only a little power comes through. My only real proof of this is my experience in 1995.

I had just retired for the night, when I heard what sounded like the buzzing of an electrical current charging through wires. I opened my eyes to see a figure forming from hundreds, perhaps thousands of tiny white dots. Stunned, I stared, uncertain what I was witnessing. The energy elongated to about six feet. Then I recognized who it was—my friend, George (not his real name) who had been very ill for some time. We argued six months previously about his lack of care for his health problems. In fact, before I left him, I said, "Next I hear you'll be dead, darn you!"

The energy buzzed for another ten seconds or so, and then faded away. I noted the time, 12:30 a.m. At about three a.m., a faint buzzing woke me again. It stopped and I felt a familiar sensation of chilled air as a spirit moved alongside me. Early the next morning, my phone rang. George's cousin, also a good friend of mine, told me he had passed away at three in the morning. He had died first around midnight she said, and was resuscitated. George was coherent enough to talk to family members before he slipped into a coma and passed away.

Happily, spirits and ghosts can re-image and manifest after death at any age they want for time does not exist, as we know it. Perhaps they wish to be remembered at a particular age and time when they were alive. I've had men show up in their World War II Army uniforms, women who died at an elderly age appear as young teens, and a child, dead before puberty, comes to me as a young adult. Even infants or toddlers who died will appear older in age. I am as curious as others how children can age in the heavens. Perhaps they were angels coming to earth to teach their parents and others something important for the living.

When the spirit comes at an age and time different how the living remembers him/her this can confuse the inquirer. Quite often I'll describe the spirit and the person who inquired will counter with, "He was older than that", and then thinking about the person, the inquirer will remark, "But yes, when he was younger he looked as you described" or "He wore glasses. Are they on him?" No, because in spirit form he doesn't need them.

At times a bit later in a session or at some time afterwards, a person remembers a detail given, as did the inquirer with the red-heeled grandmother. "I never knew my grandmother to wear red high heels," said the man when a woman in a 1950's style dress and red stilettos appeared. After the séance he recalled a black and white photograph of grandmother in high heels and wondered if they could have been red. Grandmother said they were.

Spirits can hang around for some time until they find a living person to connect with. I look at the longstanding spirit as a ghost, because she or he after a few years should really have found a peaceful rest away from the world. Sandy was one such spirit. Many years ago, before I became truly involved with, or understood, my medium abilities, I encountered a young woman named Sandy (not her real name) who was murdered execution style. My part in this sad story was through mutual friends. My brief conversation with them about Sandy's untimely death only informed me she was shot. I had no intention nor was I asked by my friends to contact Sandy. Then I had a dream about Sandy. I saw her and a man on their knees. A hand with a gun suddenly came to the back of Sandy's head. The gun went off and I awoke with a start.

She came to me with her long blonde hair flowing down a blood-soaked t-shirt. She was barefoot and in jeans. She had one hand behind her head, and the other held out asking for help in contacting her mother. I was shaking and confused. Why would someone I didn't know appear to me? I didn't know her mother Beatrice (not her real name), although my friends did. This haunting continued for a few more nights. Sandy appeared the same way with the same plea for help. You can imagine how upset I was! How could I approach a grieving mother I didn't even know to tell her about her murdered daughter? My youngest sister then telephoned crying about a ghostly woman who appeared and made the baby swing move. The ghost, said my sister, asked for me. My sister's fright made me jump into action.

Apropos for a ghost story, it was a stormy San Francisco winter day when I took my toddler to my sister's to sort out this Sandy haunting. After I calmed my sister down, we lit a candle and communicated with the spirit. Sandy wanted Beatrice to know she was sorry for not listening to her advice. Her mother needed to stop crying and thinking about how she looked at the time of death, she said. Rather Sandy wanted Beatrice to put up photos of Sandy before she fell in with a bad crowd. I telephoned a friend who put me in touch with Sandy's mother.

My friend also confirmed Sandy was shot with her boy-friend, both in the head. Beatrice was a tough cookie and not pleased to hear from me. She was angry, sad, and depressed. In her anger over he daughter's choices in life, she had already taken down Sandy's youthful photos. Regardless, I delivered my message and hurriedly left.

A week later my friend updated me, saying that Sandy's photos were up again. She handed me a thank you note from Beatrice for reuniting her with the daughter she loved and re-membered. It felt good for me to help bring a positive resolu-tion between the living and the dead.

Anther ghost who turned to me for closure (I will call her Sophie) was kidnapped and murdered. I had met her twice through her sister-in-law, a client for many years. Sophie came for psychic reading twice before going missing. The night she didn't come home, her sister-in-law called me to help locate her. I drew a picture of the man who took her, which she gave to the police. I alerted the sister-in-law if Sophie was not found by the next day, I fear she will be killed.

A month or so later Sophie's body was found where I said it would be. Three years after her death, I worked with a homicide detective and district attorney to validate the proof of the murder indictment. I directed them to each site she had been taken to by the killer with such exact details the two men were more than shocked. At one point, the detective pulled off to the side of the road stunned at the accuracy of details not known outside the police department. They didn't understand how I received the information. I told them Sophie sent it to me in dreams, which was only half true.

It didn't stop at dreams. She also came any time she pleased, sudden visions of her around my home; when I opened my closet, there she was. When I was out shopping there Sophie was in an aisle. She appeared in the white nurse uniform she wore when she was killed. Sometimes Sophie was angry and determined to get justice, and other times sad with tears running down her face. She pressed me to find her murderer, talking to me every night and throughout the day. Honestly, I felt I was going crazy. It was truly a haunting experience!

I kept in touch with her sister-in-law to give my psychic impressions to help find the killer. She would pass them on to the police. Sophie also appeared to my young son who started to talk to her too. He received invaluable clues to help locate an unexpected witness. It was a crazy three years. The man, to my knowledge is still incarcerated.

There is more to the personal side, a few years after the conviction Sophie's son came to my son's grammar school. At that time the boys didn't know the connection. Many years after, as adults they played together on a softball team. By then Sophie's son knew of my role in the case. The son asked what I knew about his mother and her death (he was brought up by his father who never spoke of the son's mother.) I wrote down everything from the psychic reading I did for Sophie over thirty years before. In it, I shared how she spoke about her great love for her brand new infant son, now this young man.

I am not sure how I could recall the information so clearly with the thousands of readings I had done since then. I think Sophie guided me. He now knows his mother was a good person who loved him and his brother dearly. She was struggling to secure a decent paying job to support her children. That was the last I heard from Sophie. May she now rest in peace.

Ghost hauntings can be fearful and stressful, but as in the cases above, they can also bring closure for some troubled souls.

There are many photographs of ghosts. Some photos are fakes. However, some appear to be real. Mostly the ghost sightings are as much of a surprise to the photographer as they would be to you or me. A classic ghostly photograph taken in 1936 of the Brown Lady of Raynham shows an eerie outline of a woman, whitely glowing as she walks down a staircase. Reportedly, it is the ghost of Lady Townshend, who was forcibly confined in the mansion by her husband until she died in 1726.

On strangerdimensions.com you can see photographs of famous ghosts caught unexpectedly. You may enjoy looking at them and reading the stories behind the ghosts to decide if they are real. On that site a photo of two friends in Manila, the Philippines, is an example of a startling ghost sighting. In it a translucent figure holds one of the smiling woman's arm. There is no information to say if it was someone they knew.

If you are interested in photographs of spirits, apparitions, orbs (more on orbs below) and other paranormal events you might want to check out Dr. Melvyn Willin's collection titled Ghosts Caught on Film: Photographs of the Paranormal and *The Paranormal Caught on Film 1 and 2*. Dr. Willin is a ghost expert, psychical investigator and the Honorary Archive Officer for the Society of Psychical Research. In it you will find photographs depicting ghosts and other extraordinary phenomena from around the world with many from Britain and some from the United States. Included are photos of the aftermath of a poltergeist's visit, and two photos of apparent levitation of a person.

For a few years ago I became involved with a paranormal investigation group called The Haunted Bay: Paranormal SF and Beyond. During an investigation of a San Francisco landmark, The Defenestration Building (closed in July, 2014), we met the ghost of a frightened woman dressed in only a full slip. She rushed toward me and the filming crew covered in blood. Her terror and quickness made us backpedal to get away. Most likely she was a victim of murder. Although, I was the only one who saw and heard her mentally, the others felt the tension. The woman came only so far down the long hallway then the image of her running toward us repeated. She was stuck in the time and place of her terror.

Later, the producer, Ying Liu and cinematographer, Matthew Abaya, returned with a camera to, hopefully, capture the ghost's image. The photographs show orbits of light and flashing streaks. The investigators thought it was inconclusive evidence because they were looking for a figure, a complete form of the woman. For me it was proof because I've seen many similar photographs of spirits and ghosts taken with different cameras. This kind of white orb light or flashes of whitish light is common when photographing spirits and ghosts. It appears as though the movement of energy is captured.

A viewer of the Defenestration video commented on the Polaroid photos of the woman with "...the Polaroid (photos) are spooky...a silhouette of a girl on the lower left...there is a set of legs in the middle... (in the Fight & Murder Hall scene) ...a face staring right at the camera and the presence behind us. I don't know if it's a bearded man or a long-haired woman..." Watch the video to decide for yourself if the shadows and lights are indeed an energy moving toward the camera crew. The Haunted Bay: Paranormal SF and Beyond video can be found on Youtube, search The Defenestration Building.

Dr. Hippolyte Baraduc a French psychical researcher, photographed milky, luminous images of globes or orbs surrounding his dying wife and in the moments after her death. Several months before his wife's death he had also photographed their young son's body nine hours after his death in 1907 with some of the same results. The images are intense as we, the viewers, realize we're looking at the dead and dying. The photos are in his book, *The Human Soul: Its Movements, Its Lights and the Iconography of the Fluidic Invisible*, and in the Time-Life book series, *Mysteries of the Unknown, Psychic Voyages*.

Only once did I witness an orb in person. A woman came to me for a past life regression through the means of hypnosis (I am a Certified Hypnotherapist). When she reached a state of relaxation a rather large, white ball manifested above her head. I was startled! It began to slowly spin and travel around the room. Since I had already prompted her to go to another time and country in the past, the woman started to talk about a lifetime. It was most difficult for me to engage with her, as I was busy watching the orb and feeling quite unnerved, having never experienced one before. Somehow I managed to ask the right questions and finally bring her back to a conscious state. When she opened her eyes the orb flew across the room and evaporated back into the crown of her head as fast as it appeared. In our conversation afterward, she said she felt her mother present, and also as though she had passed on and went to Heaven.

The question is, was the orb her mother or the spirit of the woman transcending to the heavens? I've never had a similar experience with a client.

Sometimes ghosts or spirits can be uncooperative and rather ominous. Prayers aren't going to help much, although I would still say a few just in case they calm the situation, if not you. If the ghost hauntings are very disruptive, contact a professional medium trained in dealing with such spirits so you might find relief.

Recently two people sent me videos with small orbs floating around their property. Each had security cameras in their place that picked up orbs on the film. One of the women, I'll call Ann, had contacted me a few months previously about paranormal activity in the house and asked if I could help stop, what she thought was ghosts in her home bothering the family. She already had a spiritual cleansing of her house by a medium, which had at first brought some relief of the disturbance. When it returned, it did so in full force.

Ann sent me three clips of her security film taken on different nights. The film showed her living room and front door area. In it was her husband locking up for the night. As he turns to leave the room, some circles of light appear in the forefront of the film. When he walks upstairs and disappears from view, more circles of floating lights appear. They bob around the room, flashing here and there.

At first, Ann thought maybe there was a flaw in the camera and/or film. When she showed the film to the security company they said no. They were unsure what it was and came out to replace the camera in hope that would fix the problem. It didn't stop the activity so I went to Ann's home.

Once there, I knew what was happening needed more than just one cleansing. I picked up a lot of activity in a room that had a door leading to the attic. I felt the unseen energies were not spirits of the dead returning to give a message, but rather poltergeists type entities. I attempted to contact the entities in hopes of sending them on their way and out of the house. Unfortunately, I didn't have much luck, so I then did a cleansing of the area.

In the living room area, I saw clearly a spirit of a man at the front door. After describing him to Ann and giving the name, Fred, she confirmed he was the original owner of the house. He had died in the house before she and family had bought it. I asked Fred to move into the light and onto the heavens. He laughed and said, "No," this was his home. Fred said he had earned the right to stay where he was. After I related what Fred said to Ann, she confirmed he probably did earn the right from what she heard from neighbors. He had retained ownership of the house after an acrimonious divorce. I negotiated with him to at least cease disturbing the new owners at night. Would he do that? I asked. After a few moments, I sensed a calming energy and hoped he agreed.

Ann reported back some activity in the attic had ceased to disturb her young daughter at night, and Fred did lessen his night activity too. She also learned from neighbors he was a cankerous old man, but also at times had a sense of humor so she would cajole him to let her sleep.

Before the publishing of this book I contacted Ann and found she had sold the house and moved away. I sure hope the next tenants are having better luck.

Please note when dealing with bothersome spirits who refuse to leave, negotiating can be helpful. Start with communicating, cautiously as you don't know what entity your dealing with. Begin with mentally letting the entity know you are aware of its presence. Let that settle. Then a day or so later, ask them to reveal more of whom they are, and why they're staying around. Let the ghost know how their activity or presence is not appreciated. Ask them to please move on to a more restful place than Earth. Do not become their "next best friend"—keep it cordial, but be direct and firm.

If you don't get the results you want after negotiations and/or the situation worsens, it might be time for a visiting medium to help rid you of the bothersome spirit(s), and to do a spirit/ghost house cleansing.

The other woman who contacted me about orbs was Kathryn Bazzoli, Board of Director for the Sharpsteen Museum in Calistoga, California. She sent me a video with orbs and another eerie paranormal activity caught on a security camera during closing time for the museum. In the video were flying orbs and several chairs and a table moving around a room with no evidence of anyone involved. At first I couldn't believe my eyes! I watched it several times thinking maybe I'd find a person lurking in a corner, pushing chairs and the table to the center of the room. I didn't see anyone and the furniture wasn't close to corners or walls.

The head of the security company reviewed the film and was just as baffled as Kathryn and I. The moving furniture was beyond his comprehension to why it happened. After repeated viewing and trying to figure out the reason for the orbs, he said the strange activity was not a camera malfunction or flaws in the film. What they were, he had no idea. Unfortunately, the video was not secured and no longer exists.

Months after I received the email and video, The Haunted Bay and Beyond Investigation team, and I were invited to the museum to film a ghost walk-through. We didn't witness the kind of paranormal activities as noted above, although we experienced the strong presence of spirits. And, caught on the security camera were *hot spots* of activity. When movement occurred in an area a red light would appear on the camera. While we witnessed the red dotted light, there was no living person in that area. You can see it on the Haunted Bay and Beyond Youtube video due out in early 2017.

This ghost investigation would turn out to be one of the most historically validated ones I have done to date. So much so, that Kathryn, who has written several Calistoga historical articles, and I have discussed the possibly of a book about the museum's many paranormal occurrences.

The psyche is actually more logical than not. When the conscious mind is telling you, this can't be! ––the psyche is saying, this does exist. My choice is to investigate what I psychically see, hear and sense. Think of yourself as two people, one thinking, this isn't for real, the other saying, this really is happening. I'll just shut my eyes and cover my ears and hope it all goes away. I suggest, don't try to dismiss. You can't or you can't forever because it will just come back to haunt you. Open up slowly with some caution as suggested above for you don't want a ghost moving in with you.

Become the observer. Think––let me see what's going on without deciding your experience is real, unreal, right, wrong, good or bad. When I take this position, in time proof of my ghostly/spirit experiences have merit comes from those who know facts about the dead in question, ones that I could not possibly have known.

• *Should we help send ghosts into the light?* This is a question I received from so many and although answered before, it's good to remember if you are aware of a ghost or an unhappy spirit, prayers and good thoughts can help them rest in peace and be finished with the world. Perhaps the spirits/ghosts knowing they are seen and heard, and hopefully their pains and misfortunes understood, will decide it's time to move from the physical world to a more peaceful dimension.

• *Do you think it is right to keep contacting dead people?* "To keep" are the key words. To keep calling back your dead loved ones to comfort you or help with issues such as financial problems, relationship woes, emotional support, or whatever is not right in your life isn't a good idea for the dead or you. To keep asking if they are happy, if they miss you (or whomever), to bring up how you miss them, will never be happy without them keeps both of you tied to grief. If a loved one contacts you with a message or greeting, that's fine, otherwise they are meant to rest in peace not work on the living's concerns, leave them be.

I do not encourage people to ask for messages from the dead over and over. It is we, the living, who often keep spirits attached beyond reason. When Ruth and Stan (not real names) called me for an appointment in hopes of contacting their son who had been killed a few months previously, I declined. There was no mystery how their son died––he was murdered. Ruth asked me who murdered him? While talking to her on the phone I assured her the police had the right man in custody. Due process of the law was in their favor. End of story. No charge, no appointment needed.

Ruth was insistent they meet with me. I relented because I empathized with the couple's grief and need to contact their son, Don. They had questions about why the man, a friend of Don's, had killed their son. They wanted to know if Don suffered (a reasonable and much asked question) as he lay bleeding to death? No, I said, the man had hit Don so hard on the back of the head rendering him completely unconscious. In that session, other relatives of the senior couple came forth to let them know Don was in good hands on the other side. For two more years, Ruth and Stan came back on Don's death anniversary. I wanted to give them, or more specifically Ruth, comfort. She was a persistent mother, grieving deeply for their only child. I had a difficult time being firm with stopping the sessions. Finally, it was Don who ended our meetings.

When I would say, "Dominic said..." Ruth corrected me. Dominic was Don's son—a very much alive little boy. Don said to me "Tell them there was no mistake with the name. That's whom they need to focus on. Not me." I delivered the message just as Don said it. Ruth was not happy although when I added, "Please let Don rest in peace," I saw relief on Stan's face. They never called again.

• *How do you talk to the dead? How do they talk to the living?* Let's start with how you can talk to the dead. Just simply, do it. Say her or his name, in a greeting of sorts. "Hi Jim, it's me, Mike." You can do this mentally, anywhere, anytime or you can say it aloud. The majority of spirit communication is spoken and heard telepathically; it's a telepathic or thought transference conversation. Telepathy is the most common ESP (extra-sensory perception) ability used by people and animals. If we are connected in our subconscious minds to each other as Dr. Carl Jung's concept of the collective unconscious as a universal datum states, then communication without physical means can happen. Most people are comfortable talking to their dead relatives and friends privately while others seek a medium to mediate as the go-between for the living and dead. You will learn more about this process in Chapter 9.

A medium will usually ask whom it is you wish to contact? The person inquiring will then speak the dead one's name aloud. The medium repeats the name to herself either silently or quietly as in a request for the spirit to engage with her. Often there is a moment or more of silence as communication occurs. Any forthcoming message is received mentally by the medium. In return the medium will give you the message.

The spirit's words will most likely be spoken in the language, tone and speech pattern of the medium. This is why the medium's voice usually doesn't change unless she (he) is a channel allowing for her body to be taken over by another entity for a brief time. This is not common.

The medium hears the message and interprets it usually as in third person: "Jim says, he's hanging out with your mother" rather than in the dead person as in first person. This is because she is hearing the spirit give her information, and not channeling directly.

Of course, each medium works in her or his own way. She might answer upon an inquiry as the spirit would: Mike, the inquirer asks the medium, "How are you doing Jim?" and the response comes as, "Hey Mike, I'm doing great!" instead of "Mike says to tell you he's doing fine."

If the dead person doesn't speak the language the medium does, then the medium will ask the spirit for clarification so she may translate the message properly. If the medium can't interpret the message, she most likely will tell you, or ask for your assistance by giving you what she does sense, hear or see. It could be she is experiencing communication not in words or understandable words but as seeing an image, photograph or video——a bit of sign language rather than words, if you will.

On a San Francisco ghost investigation with The Haunted Bay and Beyond, I encountered the ghost of a young girl, sick and frightened in the Defenestration building. Her family was long gone but her ghost couldn't move on. Telepathically she asked, "Where's my family? Can you help me?" I related the plea to the filming crew along with her name. Although I got the gist of what the girl said telepathically, I had difficulty translating correctly. I thought she might be German by her name and the tone of her words I heard mentally. The producer, Ying Liu, then asked the girl a question in German. Ying thought the girl would be more revealing answering in German. My non-psychic medium self said, "Oh! I don't speak German so how can I understand this conversation to translate into English?" When the ghost replied to Ying in German. Ying would translate it to English. The conversation continued between the three of us, Ying, the girl ghost and me the entire time with Ying and the girl speaking in German, me telepathically hearing it in English.

The girl ghost and I spoke telepathically in images, not all words. I saw a map of Germany and the girl pointed to a region of the country where she had come from to the United States, which I gave to Ying. There was an interaction of Ying speaking in German, stopping at times as though listening to the ghost and me answering in English. Afterward I asked Ying if her questions were answered correctly. Yes, she said. An amazing mental conversation, don't you think?

• *Why do some people see, hear, and feel spirits or ghosts while others do not?* Anyone can be aware of, and connect with, spirits or ghosts. People who are very practical and analytical are least likely to experience spirits or ghosts. To them it is not logical and reasonable. Is it their brains aren't wired as creative people's brains are? Could it be like two different professions and talents found in artists and scientists? I think there is something to that. Usually, it is the more sensitive and psychically advanced people who more easily see, hear, and feel unseen influences. Experiencing what others do not can make life uneasy for them because society, family, or religions don't usually support psychically sensitive people. Although, there are those who do not believe in this phenomenon, or are not particularity sensitive, once having experienced spirit contact they accept something outside their beliefs exists.

• *I have always seen and felt ghosts around me, even in my dreams. Some have been very scary and mean. People have told me I need help, so I'm asking you. How do I stop it?* You might not be able to completely stop spirits from communicating with you or seeing ghosts. I hear often from people who are having un-welcomed visitations from bothersome spirits and at times, vampire entities. They feel no power to stop these visitations. I'll suggest some things here and in later chapters how you can tone it down for pesky ghosts and send them away from your space.

Let me assure you that most spirit/ghost sightings and/or hauntings are quite harmless, although unnerving. Animals and the young, especially babies, see them all the time. Creative people also have a tendency to experience them maybe because they are much more aware of "unseen" energy and colors. The positive visiting spirits can be rather joyful and interesting.

You don't have to put up with the visits and manifestations. With your psychic abilities, you can curb and control them. It takes willingness, education, and guidance.

The best thing you can do for your ghostly encounters is to learn how to control the visits. That will include which spirits/ghosts you wish to communicate with, when, and how. If they bother you stand up to the ghosts and tell them forcefully to back off or to be gone! Although sorry to say, it doesn't always work that simply. Still, I'd start there. In time the spirit/ghost will listen and comply. Then again, and this is what I usually start with, negotiate with them sharing your space or bothering you. Say, "Don't make so much noise!" or "Don't touch me." Personally, my advice is to never give permission to an unwelcomed or unknown spirit to touch you!

A young man I read for had opened up to some serious vampire kind of entities that were haunting him daily. He told me he was taking the advice of his spiritual community by embracing the entities. His spiritual community encourages one to embrace an enemy with love. I researched with some of his friends who also practice this spiritual religion and concept. Love as in not judging, caring for the welfare of your enemy, not wishing ill for them. Having witnessed the young man's deterioration, emotionally, mentally and even physically, I advised the young man against embracing the kind of entities he attracted. He and I have not been in contact, but I hear through a mutual acquaintance sadly, he continues to lose control of his mind as he follows what his community advised.

Are you brave enough to ward them off? I have faced off with a few ugly, threatening entities. First thing I do is let the entity know I'm aware of it. I say, "I see you. I see you for what you are." I do this because that kind of mean-spirited thing or being, loves to play games, to hit and run, to hide then creep around to scare and hurt their victim. They don't want to be seen easily until they are ready to expose themselves once the victim is feeling frightened and weak. Yes, I've taken a few on and didn't like it at all! At all! For the seriously evil ones, I always suggest, call in someone more experienced and willing than I. Call an exorcist. That's how serious I take these kinds of entities.

If you are aware of low-grade, vampire entities please don't focus on them or engage in any way. They thrive on frightful and curious reactions from the living. When someone shows no fear (or less fearful because it *is* quite creepy) they usually just slither along to another source to haunt. If it's a poltergeist (mischievous, bothersome) entity eliminating it might need the cooperation of those sharing your living space. Many cases of poltergeist haunts involve pre-teen and teen members of the family. At that age one is highly charged emotionally and poltergeist seem to be attracted to their energy.

Be it a poltergeist or a dark, vampire entity and you are faced with an on going, disruptive, and possibility harmful entity, consult a medium educated and experienced with these kinds of disturbances. They are best equipped to handle the situations.

Do not try to do it on your own as you can exasperate the entities. Dealing with either of the above entities will no doubt disturb your peace of mind, upset your emotional well- being, and in time drain your physical health. Please know they often don't go away easily, and can actually create more chaos.

If spirits and ghosts are continuing interests to you, I highly recommend educating yourself about your psychic abilities.

With knowledge you can know how and when to *turn them on* —— that is communicate with your beloved spirit family and friends——and when to *turn them off* ——close the mental or psychic doors until you are ready to open them. It's your decision, even when the spirits keep knocking at your psychic door. I do know some are very bothersome and it becomes difficult to keep them at bay. We'll go more into that later.

In Chapter 12 take June's ESP Quiz to learn about your own psychic abilities. Think about joining groups with other psychics/mediums to know you are not alone. Classes and workshops are a good way to meet like-minded others. Attend such learning events as meditation groups, aura reading, Reiki, developing ESP abilities, and like that. I continue to benefit from events and just being with other psychics. In time as you become comfortable with your abilities look for positive ways to being a comfort to others.

In my book, *The Timeless Counselor: The Best Guide to a Successful Psychic Reading,* I give an example of a woman named Kathy who had strong mediumship abilities and how she truly felt she was going insane. After the reading she took my ESP Development and Tarot classes. In time, she accepted her abilities and returned to her sense of wonderment. You don't have to be a helpless victim of ESP. In Chapter 9 - Mediums, I will give more suggestions about cleansing your energy and space.

• *Do most spirits cross over and just a few stay behind and if so, for how long do they stay with us, the living?* Almost all spirits cross over within a short period of time after death. If they died of old age or suffered from a lingering illness most likely they welcomed death, glad to be relieved from pain and illnesses.

In fact, elderly people go between the worlds, so to speak, for often up to a few years before death. They visit the other side when nodding off into a sleep state. While there, they visit loved ones who have gone on before them. Awake they will speak about their departed relatives and friends more often than usual. When they do die and cross over it is easier for them to go. I know this because I've talked to many elderly and dying patients who tell me how they've been visiting the other side in their dreams. When giving a psychic reading to elderly and gravely ill clients I see their loving spirits surrounding them. My clients happily acknowledge they too feel and see them.

After a sudden death, such as a heart attack, stroke, accident or murder the spirit often lingers around earth a bit longer. They are as stunned as those left behind, by the quick ejection from the body. They mourn their separation from life until they can accept the transition.

Suicide can bring a mixed transition. The spirit wants to rest from the chaos and pain of their life. When I communicate with the spirit of suicide victims sadly much of the same emotional and mental pain continues in the afterlife. Their questions of why they are still in pain and how can they get away from it remain unanswered in the spirit world. People who have chosen to end suffering from long and painful illnesses find some rest soon after leaving. Ultimately peace of spirit does happen. If it doesn't find peace, the spirit can stay earthbound searching for relief.

There is also remorse——the guilt over those they left behind. That too must come to a peaceful resolution for the spirit to transition to a higher state of being. My advice is as before, pray for the souls of your loved ones who found life too painful. To the best of your ability forgive them for leaving before a healing could be found and communicate that to your loved one. Your prayers will help them find the peace they sought while alive.

• *Do they watch us, or have they got much more important things to do "on the other side"?* For a period of time a loved one will stay in contact with us. Maybe they are concerned for our sorrow. As it is for us, the living, separation from an important relationship, from a shared life with a person, is not easy to end. In time, most spirits accept they are dead and no longer a part of this world. They move on to the next plane.

The Rosicrucian Order AMORC teaches when we die we are met by a panel or board of Higher Beings. One of these beings is our archangel who came with us at birth and is with us when we are dying to help us transition to the other side. Along with the panel, we examine our life, what we did, learned, wish to atone for. We also discover what we need to learn to become whole. Becoming whole means we release that which pains us mentally and emotionally. Our physical pains are examined and shown to us how they relate to our thoughts and emotions (see Louise Hay, *You Can Heal Your Life*). With these insights we transcend to a state of grace and pure love. If you would like to learn more about the order please review at www.amorc.org.

When we are whole, we accept ourselves just as we are. With this acceptance comes the awareness that we have a choice to change. We are peaceful and joyful spirits and understand our purpose whether we reincarnate (come back to live in a physical body) or stay on the "other side" to work for the betterment of humanity. We view both sides of relationships and situations without judgment and willingly atone for deeds which hurt not only others but ourselves. The lessons we learn on the other side prepare us for a return to life to complete the cycle of becoming whole.

Some spirits have told me they are busy mending relationships where anger or misunderstandings kept them apart during life. Others have told me their job on the other side is to watch over abused children to keep them safe or in some way help them. Or, they are learning for a future incarnation on earth to assist in the balance of nature. After our time with the panel we meet upon crossing over there is a reunion with those who have passed before us. They encourage and contribute to our healing.

Mitch Albom's novel, *The Five People You Meet in Heaven*, is a story about Eddie's life and those he met along the way. When Eddie dies, he meets the five most influential people who both made a difference in his life and those he influenced the most. He learns understanding and resolution needed for a peaceful rest. The story is a reminder that after death we continue to have opportunities to learn and evolve into compassionate and wise beings.

• *Can pets that have passed away communicate with us?* We animal lovers dread the moment when our beloved pets—our companions—die. We fear our pets are lost to us forever. The grief can be as powerful as when we lose a person. Communication from a pet can be just as emotional as one with the spirit of a human loved one, and the reasons we want contact with them are the same. We want to know if they made the transition okay. We ask if our pets are now pain free. We wonder if they miss us like we miss them? Our beloved animal companions stay close to us in spirit for as long as they feel we need their comfort. They will not want to leave you until you are more emotionally settled, or have adopted a new pet.

The energy of a pet doesn't dissipate quickly after death. Animals are spirits, just as all life is spirit. Since we share the earth, it is easy to believe we exist in the spirit world together. They have a strong spirit presence and in my experience, can often be felt easier than human spirits can. Perhaps it's the pureness of the animal spirit, which is not as complicated as humans. You might actually smell the pet as though it were in the room with you. You could sense your pet is watching you, turn in a direction, and catch out of the corner of your eye, a fluff of color, or the tail of your "pet ghost" dashing out of the room.

When my cat, and later my dog, passed away, some clients upon entering my office, would look around and asked, "Where's the (cat or dog)?" I would tell them they've gone on——died." Surprised, the clients remarked, "But I feel him (or her)." Were they psychic? Did they feel or sense the animal was still in the room? Perhaps to a degree they are because they certainly were sensitive to the energy of my animals.

People ask me if animals can communicate with us after death. I assure you, contact and communication with your pets can happen. During séances as well as in private psychic sessions I have shared many messages with teary-eyed pet guardians from their beloved animal friends. The spirits of dogs or cats commonly appear without an inquiry. Usually, they come to sit by a particular person. If not, after I describe the animal, someone happily claims it as her or his pet.

As animal guardians (owners) know, they do not communicate in exactly the same way humans do. We humans use words and our pets do not. Although animals do make sounds to communicate, most of their messages come through body language. My pets made it plain to me when they wanted something. My dogs gave me that "special look" when they wanted a treat or a walk. If that didn't work, a short bark or whine got my attention. My cats stared at me intensely until I could no longer ignore them. If I tried to, they'd jump on me or wrap their bodies around my legs herding me to what they wanted.

Knowing your pet's body language will help you to create a closer relationship with your pet. I recall a horse whisperer's advice, "Don't try to get your horse to understand your language, you learn to understand its language" and therefore, I watched how horses used their body to get their point across to other horses. A toss of the head meant, "move along or get out of my way." Flattened ears declared, "I'm not happy! Better watch out!" And, of course, they have different whinnies to tell you their needs.

When you communicate with your spirit pets, you will receive images, actions and/or hear their animal sound. If communication is through a pet medium, she or he will receive from the pet particular information to identify contact with your pet has been made. The medium might see your pet's personal habit or a favorite belonging.

Pet mediums are certainly one method for communicating, but I encourage you to do it on your own as well. Sit quietly in the room you and your pet favored. You can place a photograph (your favorite one) in front of you or hold it. Take several deep breaths to relax. Say your pet's name a few times. Relax deeper and let your mind drift to an image of her or him, maybe a special playtime, or look at that photo. Bring back that loving feeling: Imagine stroking your pet, feel the fur and warmth beneath your fingertips. You could feel the wet nose of your dog nudging your hand. You might hear the purr of your cat. There is no doubt you will experience the presence of your pet as you move into the memories.

What will you want to know about your pet? If your pet was in pain, you'll want to know if he/she is free of it now. If you feel guilt, a common grief feeling especially when having to humanely euthanize a pet, you might want to know if you are forgiven. Mentally, ask the question. Be still. Allow images to *come to you*. In other words, don't force an answer. Rather enjoy the moment of relaxing as you open to what comes to your mind. Relax, smile. I'm sure you will see a happy pet face or feel warmth of love in your heart, just as your pet would want you to. If nothing comes immediately, the answer will manifest later. If you become emotionally overwhelmed, take a break. Once you've calmed down, redo the exercise.

Your pet can appear to you spontaneously. It might be when you think all connection is lost, as I did when my beloved Phoebe, a sixteen-year-old white Standard Poodle, died. As a one-year-old she had come into my life unexpectedly. I was at an emotionally low point and fearful of my financial future. This state caused a frantic energy within me. I couldn't rest properly. Phoebe was an easy, calm dog who would cringe when I was in that state. I remember looking at her in the corner trembling and decided I wasn't being fair to her. She taught me the value of enjoying simple times in life, to take long walks, and not to worry because she loved me no matter what.

At the time of her death I had another dog, an adorable Pit Bull mix named Gunner, yet I grieved heavily the loss of Phoebe. A year after her death while walking Gunner I had the strangest spirit occurrence––even for me! A blonde woman dressed in all white walked toward us. Later, when recounting the story, I would say she reminded me of Daryl Hannah, tall and slender. As the young woman passed by us, she smiled sweetly and said, "Don't you know me? I'm Phoebe."

I was so stunned I continued to walk on, unable to digest what just occurred. At some point, I turned to look back and saw no one. How did she know my Phoebe's name? Could Phoebe really have returned as a human? Was she truly an angel as she had been to me in life? I chose to believe Phoebe was indeed an angel that manifested as a dog to help heal me emotionally. Our pets teach us so much, don't they?

Animals come into our life to bring comfort, to make us laugh, protect us, and to share our adventures. Our deceased pets would, and do, wish that once they have died we find the same comfort and friendship from another pet. Thank your pet ghost for all he, or she, gave you and bless them to be free to run (or lay in the sun) over the rainbow.

• *What about "evil spirits?" Do they really exist like in the movie The Exorcist? If they do, have you seen any and did they scare you?*

From my brief experience with harmful, bothersome entities, I am certain they exist like in the movie. It does scare me. I do everything to distance myself from those kinds of ghostly entities. I know my limits. When asked to go to certain haunted locations, I check my psyche to see if I can do any good. A while ago, I was asked by the paranormal investigation group to go to locations where the infamous Zodiac victims were murdered. I declined, not willing to feel, see, hear or be part of that. Later, I learned the medium channeled through one victim's horrific experience of her murder in detail. The medium displayed so much anguish that the group made a wise choice not to air the film out of respect for the living members of the victim.

Even though I'm cautious, my latest San Francisco ghost haunting video in the famous Defenestration building (closed July, 2014) provided low-grade entities and a frightening murder scene, as seen in a video of The Haunted Bay Paranormal Investigations featured on Youtube. That experience was nothing like my first visit to a true "possessed house" in Jamaica. A group of Jamaicans flew me there for readings and lectures. It turned into an incredible journey! I was humbled by how the people treated me like royalty. My time was spent with new clients, students, and wonderfully interesting people.

I toured Jamaica as a guest of the residents, taken places where white people seldom go. A valuable lesson came from the most memorable event; do not mess with evil or "vampire" entities. A handsome elderly gent was scheduled for a reading. Right away, I picked up he was a healer, a doctor in fact. Next I saw his wife very ill. He confirmed his wife, Violet, had cancer. They had been to New York to see specialists and had little hope for a cure or recovery. What plagued her, and him most, were the demons who attacked his wife in their home. I didn't really believe this. I knew there were mean spirits, and even trouble-making poltergeists but I had no experience with demons. For a psychic, I am rather skeptical. Show me and then I believe it can be. Against my better judgment but encouraged by my hosts, I agreed to visit his wife at their home. My skepticism turned to belief. It was July in the Caribbean—hotter than you know what!

When I entered the home, I felt a chill grow inside of me. Right away, I walked to a closed door and announced, "Here! Here is where they come in!" The husband flung open the door and I entered a hellish experience. The room felt like an ice locker although it was an old enclosed porch. It had been off, what I learned later, the original kitchen, which sat above an underground stream of water, a conduit for energies, good, bad or ugly. An odor like garbage rose from the floor and out of the walls. I couldn't breathe. My energy faltered. I was dizzy. Slapped, punched, pinched––my body was attacked by unseen entities. I moaned and groaned, fought my ridiculous behavior. After all, I tried to tell myself I'm a practical psychic! I started to fall. The man grabbed my arm and led me out.

Once I was composed, he took me to meet his bedridden wife. As soon as I entered her room, growling came from her bedside. It wasn't her, but something in the room I couldn't see. She lay with her eyes closed under many blankets, too many for the stifling heat in the room. I could see bruises on her face. The doctor had told me she was bruised all over from the attacks of the entities. Suddenly, I was attacked again. It felt like wet towels stinging my face, my arms, and my body. Then I got angry, yelped in pain and screamed, "STOP IT YOU EVIL THINGS!" They did. The room was still and silent. The wife opened her eyes. I sat next to her and said, "Yes, you are being attacked by evil entities on your property." The couple was grateful someone finally believed them. I did pick up her cancer was exacerbated by these "things." I could offer little help to these nice people, as I had not enough knowledge of, or experience in, exorcisms. The vapors of these dark entities came up from the land the house was built on. Who knows what happened there? Was it a burial site? A place where evil practices took place? My parting advice to them was to move far away from that house, the land. They said, no. It was their home. I was bruised from the attack and if I had known I'd be talking about it, I would have photographed the marks. Then, however, I wanted to put it behind me. After leaving Jamaica I never communicated with the couple again.

• *What is being possessed like?* Possession isn't a subject I readily discuss. In my more than forty years' experience with the paranormal things logic told me could never happen has happened to me. I'm not sure if people are really possessed demons or if they suffer from grave mental illnesses and disorders, or if their behavior is caused by drugs.

Many over history have believed in demonic possession. The belief continues today, with deadly consequences, in such places as Africa. Demonic possession is thought to be the possession of an individual by a malevolent supernatural entity commonly called Satan, the devil or a demon. When a person is possessed, they experience pronounced personality changes for the worse. The person's voice and facial expressions often noticeably change. They might speak in a foreign language they couldn't speak before. They might become violent, spit, urinate on themselves, or have convulsions (i.e. epileptic seizures or fits). A person believes a spirit or demon entity has taken away his or her free will and is in control of her or his mind or body. He/she might think, "I've gone mad," or "A supernatural power of devil has overtaken me!"

If you are worried you, or someone you know, are possessed please speak to a licensed therapist or your spiritual leader who preferably has knowledge. Do not automatically think of possession unless you have reason to believe you or another has become vulnerable to it.

• *If spirits and entities can possess people, how does it happen?* It is thought these evil entities find a way in through weakness in the person's behavior. People worn down by illnesses or depression are targets. Low-grade, or evil entities can be attracted to one who dabbles in the occult and performs certain rituals without proper education and guidance. Again, this is why I discourage young people's participation in séances or ghost hunts. They are much too vulnerable, too impressionable and not cautious enough to make safe or wise decisions when a potential dangerous situation is presented.

A National Institutes of Health study reports the complete development and region of the brain that inhibits risky behavior is not fully developed until a person reaches their mid-twenties. If the young person has demonstrated strong psychic abilities and easily communicates with spirits what is needed is an experienced and knowledgeable mentor. My advice is to encourage the young person to *not* attempt to explore on her/his own.

Unlike one who is channeling spiritual knowledge, the possessed person has no control over the entity that has taken over. Their changed behavior will persist until the spirit is forced to leave the victim, usually through a form of exorcism performed by a trained exorcist. According to the website Oddee.com "… the Catholic church performs thousands of exorcisms each year, and Pope Francis has said he believes that Satan is real, and that the battle against evil is one that he must fight every day."

Quite a few books (i.e. *Devils of Loudun* by Aldous Huxely) and movies (several on the well- known Amityville haunting) have titillated those who like a horror thrill. My introduction to demonic possession was the 1973 movie *The Exorcist*, based on Peter Blatty's 1971 novel of the same title. The movie, inspired by the 1949 exorcism by Roland Doe, deals with the demonic possession of a 12-year-old girl and her mother's attempts to win back her child through an exorcism conducted by two priests. The movie scared me enough that I stay clear of any area or person who might be possessed, just in case it was a real occurrence. As mentioned earlier, the only times I came close to encountering low-grade, vampire entities up close was in Jamaica and The Defenestration Building.

I have read about all kinds of symptoms used to determine if a person is possessed. Many seem to be signs of depression or a mental disorder. Some seem to be normal behavior especially with teenagers. Most of the symptoms can be related to medical or psychological conditions, but some of them do fall outside the realm of explainable science. There are a very few examples of what a person might display if possessed such as noticeable changes in the person's attitude and behavior, usually hostile. Cursing a lot when it is out of character for that person. A sudden aversion to religious objects develops. A person self-mutilates. An obsession with the occult takes over their life. He or she becomes violent. The person hurts animals and/or animals appear to be frightened of the person for no apparent reason. There are multiple voices coming from the person at the same time.

We have to wonder if serial killers are mentally defective or possessed by demons. Some of the most notorious certainly appear to be possessed by evil: The Zodiac Killer; Tsutomu Miyazaki known as The Human Dracula. Ted Bundy, The Crazy Necrophilia; Jack the Ripper (Whitechapel Murderer); Jeffrey Dahmer: The Milwaukee Cannibal; Josef Mengele, "The Angel of Death."

This is to name but only a few of these frightening killers. I am most interested in, and following the continual and most fascinating study of the brain. I know in time we will learn how it works with startling results about these kinds of criminals. The study will show how defects in the brain are the cause malfeasance, but then again how and from what source are these defects formed?

• *Do you believe in vampires and can they really suck the blood out of you?* When I read this question, I thought of people I've known personally and professionally, who seemed to suck the blood (my energy) out of me with their on-going problems and whining. I'm sure you have those people in your life too.

One of my favorite spirit communication books, *Letters From the Other Side* by Mary Blount White has a chapter "False Messages from Harpies and Vampires." It is about vampire entities also described as low-grade entities. Ms. Blount says these are lower than ghosts who once housed a physical body. White says these types of low-grade, energy sucking entities take a toll on the body, mind, and spirit while often being very engaging. They have such a strong love for life they fight death, and refuse to believe they are not alive. They can have a powerful hate for all people; cling to people or things they loved, or disliked and live on the vitality and magnetism of living people. These entities tend to reincarnate at the first opportunity, quite recklessly, and create another chaotic existence. Some of these low-grade entities never had human form and come from the evil energy of the minds of people who were, and are, destructive. If you are healthy and strong of body and mind, chances of a mean or a low-grade entity attaching to you are not likely. They like the old, the ill, the gullible, children, the overly emotional persons and those who can't easily protect themselves. There is an antidote for these types of spirits or beings says Ms. White: Simple loving, pure, and positive thoughts, kind words and a willingness to help others who are down on their luck are the cure. An excerpt from the chapter in "Letters" reads: "It takes love, and those who care, to make the chain strong enough to carry past the borderland of darkness where spirits live who love to deliver false messages. We sometimes have to fight to keep the harpies and vampires away from those we love, because our people are so ignorant they allow themselves to drift below the boundary, one where we always conquer." [*sic*]

I recommend be mindful of your thoughts creating chaos and unhappiness; endeavor not to let dark, angry or fearful ones prevail. It is in this state one can attract negative people and experiences as well as be open to low-grade entities. If you find you cannot turn away from negative thoughts, seek help from positive family and friends, a religious advisor or psychotherapist.

• *Have you ever heard of bad ghosts attaching themselves to you?* It can happen and indeed is called attachment. The more involved you are with spirit and ghost communication the more likely you will attract ghosts at some time. This can result in not only nightmares but in a decline of health and false messages. You might be communicating with one spirit while a less than nice one takes over. False messengers and low-grade energies can also reach you through the Ouija Board. Not having positive spirit connections with the Ouija Board, I never encourage people to "play" with it. Once again this is why I don't encourage the unprepared, gullible or young to communicate with ghosts. Training, education, and a guide to the spirit world can protect the go-between (medium) from these kinds of attachments.

It is easy to become vulnerable to low-grade entities when one becomes tired and worn down. I enjoy my spirit communication, but I also know when it's time to rest to avoid false messengers, as best I can. One of the reasons I no longer work on murder cases with the police is because it's too emotionally and spiritually taxing. This along with the violent deaths absolutely can leave me vulnerable to attachments. Self-protection is *very* important. You will read more about protection in Chapter 6, Self-Protection.

My first experience with an attachment was with a man from the United States who had lived in Africa for a few years. He came for a reading because of repeated failed professional attempts since his return from Africa. I picked up African artifacts surrounding him. He confirmed yes, he had brought back several. I then "saw" psychically one of those pieces had a hostile spirit lurking within it. It looked like a dark, greenish glob of energy with no ability to verbally communicate, although it sent off strong bad vibes. The glob had attached to the side of the man's face. When I told him what and where I saw it, he confirmed that on that side he had been having horrible earaches and a terrible shoulder pain. Although he had seen several doctors, nothing was found physically to be the cause. I recommended Reiki and along with a few rituals to remove the attachment. In time, he returned to good health and professionally became successful once again. Why did this happen? My psychic take was he was a victim of a nasty, low-grade entity that attached itself to the wood from which the piece was made. It didn't matter who bought it they would have suffered too.

I had another case of attachment to a Native American client. The young woman had begun to suffer from severe migraines. She was under doctor care, but her belief was something other than a physical cause was the reason for her headaches. Recently, she had visited a gravesite and believed a negative spirit had followed her home and was worried she was possessed by it. I saw energy attached to the side of her head as well as to the back of her neck. It was not deeply embedded into her body therefore she was not possessed in the way described in an earlier answer. This entity did not appear like the man's had. It had an appearance of a misshapen grotesque face. Indeed, something ugly had followed her out of the gravesite. At that time, I had started hands on healing classes so I laid my hands on her head in hopes of easing some of the pain while pulling out the attachment. She finally removed the attachment completely with the help of her medicine man and time in a sweat lodge. Later, I read in Chinese medicine it is thought evil spirits enter through the back of the neck to bring illnesses to the body.

From these two psychic experiences, I have learned, once again, not everything in the paranormal world can be explained through science. My life as a professional medium has taught me, do not dwell upon the dead nor grieve too long. Do not open your heart and soul for all spirits, ghosts and entities to come into you. Do not "play" with contacting spirits and ghosts.

• *Sometimes, I'm thrilled when I feel a pull from walking past a building where there are spirits, and other times it totally creeps me out. How can I deal with that, and calm myself?* As with living people we enjoy and others make our skin crawl, ghost energy is the same. If you feel uncomfortable, stay away. When you're sensing something is not good in that space, don't encourage it. Calm yourself, but do not let a ghost chase you away. They thrive on fear. "Ghost busting" or exorcism, or any kind of interaction or communication with a low-grade entity or ghost is not for the weak of mind and body, or fearful. Under certain circumstances like engaging with a powerfully dark, malicious entity, even those with knowledge in parapsychology, can experience negative results. (Parapsychology is the investigation of para-normal and psychic phenomena.) A whiff of fear and one or more can attach to your terror. If the pull is too great and you need to investigate, first ground yourself by taking a few easy deep breaths. Consider saying a prayer and take a moment to imagine you in a warm, white light bubble of safety. Think of energy going down to the bottom of your feet and running back up and out of the top of your head. Feel mentally clear. Be aware of how you feel and calm any area in your body that feels tense. Tell yourself to be calm, safe, and peaceful. Say it a few times as well as "I am only open to positive, loving spirits who wish to communicate with me." Do not let your imagination run away with you.

• *What does the Bible say about spirit communication and people like you?* This question has been asked of me many times. It is an important concern for those with strong religious beliefs who fear such attempts at communication only brings around evil entities. Numerous times, I've been told I'm going against God's teaching. I'm often asked by religious people if I believe in God and Jesus or am I a Satan follower? I do believe in God. I do follow teachings of Jesus to be compassionate and peaceful. My upbringing was in a very strict Catholic household and I went to parochial school. There are those belonging to churches that come to me asking for total secrecy because they fear their congregation might learn about our talk. They tell me their stories of seeing or hearing spirits and like all others who have experienced the same, want validation they are not going against God's will or going crazy. I share my experiences and knowledge without swaying them from their religious beliefs.

I've had sessions with people from almost every walk of life and varied religious practices and tried to help them understand their spirit experiences. People with psychic abilities cannot stop just because they are forbidden or warned against it. It's part of their psyche. The best approach to dispel misunderstandings and superstitions about psychic phenomena is education and research. Parapsychology is not a new study, although more researchers and investigators have become involved in it. It is being taken more seriously like any other scientific research. One of the leading and best known psi (psychic or ESP) researches in the U.S. are conducted at the Rhine Research Center, (once associated with Duke University Durham, North Carolina). Rhine Executive Director John Kruth said, "We are scientists...trying to improve on the science as we move along...We're talking about everything from near death experiences. This is also where spirits, haunting and ghosts fit in."

Professional paranormal investigation and research groups seek to separate facts from fiction and about phenomena of spirit communication and ghostly encounters. Paranormal Research Organization states that they are committed to "create a network of knowledgeable and ethical field researchers and investigators who conduct field research and investigation of psychic and so-called paranormal phenomena and experiences." They also are dedicated to "creating ethical guidelines on how they conduct their work and interact with people who claim to have had paranormal experiences." Michigan State Paranormal Investigations (michigan-paranormal.com/), a non-profit group, write they too are committed to debunking claims knowing "everything is not paranormal and everything cannot be explained." Scientific studies certainly can dispel superstitions and misunderstandings, although it might not be enough for those who have religious beliefs, which differ from results. The human psyche and paranormal experiences do not so easily fit into scientific explanations. In this book as well as my other guide, *The Timeless Counselor: The Best Guide to a Successful Psychic Reading,* I advise readers how to approach and avoid unethical people who might abuse their position as psychics and mediums.

But I am not surprised! Even Satan can disguise himself as an angel of light. So, it is no wonder his servants can also do it by pretending to be godly ministers. In the end they will get every bit of punishment their wicked deeds deserve. 2 Corinthians 11:14-15.

It's not only Christianity that warns against interaction between the dead and the living. Buddhism, for another, also teaches not to become involved with ghostly interaction. And, I understand why. It is true when the doors, or veils, open between the two existences––life and death––a Pandora's Box of uncontrollable situations can bring great grief. In what is called the *astro or astral existence, world,* or *plane* negative, low-grade entities, and sometimes, evil spirits exist along with the energy of the dead. They can, and will, fool you into believing they are good or are the spirit you desire to contact. In this existence, your hopes and fears manifest back to you and true contact with the spirit can become confused with personal thoughts.

More about the astro or astral plane: classical, medieval, oriental, and esoteric philosophies and mystery religions claim it is a world of celestial spheres or a plane of existence where the soul of the living cross into via the astral body on the way to being born and after death, and is generally believed to be where angels, spirits or other immaterial beings reside.

When men tell you to consult mediums and spiritists, who whisper and mutter, should not a people inquire of their God? Why consult the dead on behalf of the living? Isaiah 8:19.

The Bible teaches spiritual guidance should be sought from God alone for He has provided everything we need for this life and all answers to what we seek will come through the Holy Spirit and Jesus Christ. Most know when they are not acting in accordance for the good of themselves and others. Your conscious is a guide that you are listening to *The Word of God*. In the Rosicrucian teachings you are encouraged to connect to the *The Master Within*. The Master Within connects to your inner wisdom and knowledge as well as the God of your heart. Doing so will provide you with the necessary information and knowledge to make good decisions.

Psychology tells us we have the intelligence necessary for solving our issues once we trust ourselves. I agree, and also know we need to be taught (or re-taught) to connect to our own wisdom. Unfortunately, most of us were not taught to seek answers within, but rather to be dependent on others. Remain open to hearing others' thoughts, but also listen to your own inner wisdom. Prayer and meditation will give you the opportunity to connect with the God of your heart and mind so you might hear what is necessary for you to be wise in your dealings, worldly and otherworldly.

In upcoming chapters I discuss what we hope to gain or learn by talking to the dead. Mainly, the living want to know if the dead are at peace, happy as well as to appease any guilt about not doing enough before their loved one died.

Do not turn to mediums or seek out spiritists, for you will be defiled by them. I am the LORD your God. Leviticus 19:31.

The laws in Leviticus commanded mediums, sorcerers and diviners be stoned to death if found among God's people. It was forbidden to engage in black magic or sorcery, divination, or otherwise. At that time, and even today, superstitions and fears made the unknown evil or bad. There was less access to education about mystics, mediums and psychic abilities. The warnings in the Bible were about the abuse by psychics/mediums and those posing as such who took advantage of people seeking guidance.

I once asked my parish Monsignor if what I did was against Catholic teachings. He answered with these questions, "Did I tell people I knew best, better than God or Jesus?" and "Did I encourage people to listen only to me and not to seek answers through prayer?" I answered, "No, I did not." In fact, I told him that I encourage and teach people to seek answers within themselves, to connect to their greater intelligence, and to seek guidance from their spiritual or religious advisors, or a psychotherapist, if their pain is great.

He responded, "Then what you are doing is helping people and keep doing it."

Strongly held religious beliefs will never be changed by another, nor should they be. If a person realizes there is more to be learned about spirituality, then good. My hope is people will keep open minds, without prejudice, and respect the experience and knowledge of others outside of their own experiences.

The goal of this book is to teach how to safely and wisely interact with the spirits of the dead. Obsessive or continual focus on spirit communication or ghostly encounters is not healthy. If you do engage in this interest, through my book I can advise you how to care for your spiritual, mental, emotional and physical well-being.

• *When I am at a séance and I see and hear spirits, but I'm shy about sharing it, can I share the messages without disturbing the flow of the séance or medium's own messages?* I would hope the medium would be open to you sharing, but I would ask beforehand if it would disturb the flow. The medium might have a time to share during the séance. I suggest you ask before the séance begins if participants are allowed to contribute messages and when can that be done. Although it can be disturbing to mediums if they are receiving messages, perhaps in trance, it can benefit another participant. I handle this by announcing before the séance not all spirits talk to the medium, but rather choose another individual. If anyone receives a message or is contacted by a spirit, please share. During séances I say, "Now is the time to share." At that time the participants sharing doesn't interfere with my messages.

At one of my séances a student of mine who had never experienced spirit communication blurted out, "There's a man here with a cap on. No wait! He said it was a bonnet. A tam." She paused as though listening and then proceeded, "The message is for you, June. He's saying you'll know what that means." I did, it was my father who had died suddenly about ten years before that séance and long before this woman became a student of mine. She did not know my father, our history or how he looked but described each aspect of him exactly. She proceeded to give me a message from my father. Needless to say, she was overwhelmed how a spirit spoke through her. Her name is Suzette Standring, a columnist and author of two non-fiction books and one of the most "let me see for myself" persons I ever met with a most inquisitive, analytical mind. I assured her how appreciative I was of the message because I had wanted to make contact with him.

If you are too shy to share during the séance, please do so afterward with the one you believe the message is for or with the medium to pass on to the person.

• *Where can I go to find ghosts? Are there special places they haunt?* For me, the dead walk all around us. For the novice ghost hunter, it's far more likely you will find the spirit in old buildings with some local history. Some of these buildings may be closed down like churches, military bases, schools, courthouses, and hospitals; places that had a lot of activity. Of course, graveyards are always good for a ghost or two sightings. When I saw a funeral home in my neighborhood where I had attended a few services had sold and condos built on the site, I thought, Oh boy! I bet the new residents will bump into a few spirits. See Chapter 12, Ghost Hunts for more about places to find lingering ghosts and how to prepare for a ghost hunt.

• *Do fear and anger still come through, or are most of the spirits civil when summoned?* I have channeled angry and unpleasant spirits repeating their exact words along with their tones and attitudes. I recall a young man (dead at sixteen from a motorcycle accident) disgruntled about missing some organs. He said the pain was great. I reminded him he was dead and no longer attached to a physical body. The pain was his experience of the crash. He argued no, the pain was because he wasn't physically whole. He wanted his liver back. I told this to the person asking. Later I learned she was the recipient of one of his organs and upset at his anger. I introduced the young man to the woman and reminded him in a way he continued to live and give life. He still had a purpose, which was to be happy for helping her continue with life. Before he left the session, he calmed down knowing he would not be forgotten.

When we die our attitudes and actions remain as they were in life until our transformation or transcendence of spirit has occurred. I've had very funny characters at times with risqué stories for the living. Jokesters in life continue as comedians in death.

Salty the sailor was one. During a session in an old San Francisco home, one of the participants screeched, "He's touching my thigh!" "Who?" I asked. "Salty," she declared. Since I wasn't picking him up, I asked the woman to describe him. He was an old man dressed in a sea captain's uniform and hat. The woman who lived in the house knew no one named Salty nor did anyone else. He went around each woman and hugged or touched legs and more! Salty was crafty. Every time I asked a question, he'd ask a question back––Have you been to sea, ye young wench? Do ye like the roll of the waves? The session became so disruptive with laughter, squeals and women jumping up in fear that we ended it early. Two days later, I learned from the woman who lived in the house when her landlady knew who the old sailor was. Salty, was her uncle's nickname. He was a sea captain with the reputation of being a ladies' man and a great jokester.

My experience is most spirits reach a peaceful state within a short time and come back to greet the living calm and happy. As said before, when people pass over to the other side their awareness grows in their own time, not our earthly time, and if they do return to communicate they usually come across as less angry, more understanding, and wiser.

• *What is the purpose of spirit communication?* The purpose of a spiritualist meeting or a séance is to receive information to help gain knowledge, wisdom and guidance. What is received could be to a validation or response to one's inquiry from a spirit, or at times a Divine Being such as God, Allah, Buddha, Goddess, guardian angel, spirit teachers and guides.

• *Do all of us here on Earth have guides who exist in the spirit plane for us?* This is my belief. There is a guardian angel assigned to us at birth and who stays with us throughout our lifetime. This angel cannot always keep us safe because we are born with "free will." That is we can and do choose to do one thing or another. It is thought our guardian angel stays as close as he or she can while we are young and somewhere along the line, as we become young adults, steps back for us to learn our life lessons and mature. The angel returns later during our senior years and/or at the time of your death. At various times throughout life and most likely when our guardian angel steps back, we can encounter spiritual teachers and/or guides according to what we want to learn. A particular spiritual teacher or guide will come to us when we request their assistance. Such a being can also be useful as a go-between like a medium when you want to communicate with a dead loved one.

• *Why do spirits want to communicate with us?* If spirits asks to communicate then they have a message for you. Once again, communication can occur during in dreams, or a sudden flash of thought as though you heard a voice or mentally saw your dead person.

I have experienced beautiful positive spirit energies with messages of love and encouragement. Whenever we are emotionally attached to a person and that person dies, we, and often they, are not ready to end the relationship. A spirit stays connected to the living to comfort and answer their concerns. Maybe the spirit wants to support, advise and/or let you know they made it to the other side and all is well. The spirit may make a request for prayers, especially if the death was violent or the person had been depressed, and does not have divine rest. We can ask our loved ones on the other side to help us on our life path by giving us certain knowledge, support, protection, and/or guidance.

Most spirits validate themselves through personal and individual information only you will identify. Please understand, not all spirits communicate when petitioned. Perhaps the spirit will contact you at another time or in another way than words. The spirit might not speak to you in a waking state. Your answer might come in a dream, through another living person or a symbol like a bird landing close to you at the moment you think of your loved one.

• *I believe my mother, who died twenty years ago, continues to help guide me as she did when alive. Do you think she is my guardian angel as*

I do? You are truly a blessed daughter to have had such a loving mother that you wish to keep alive in your heart and life. Perhaps you read my answer to the question, *Do they watch us, or have they got much more important things to do on the other side"?* In it, I discuss how shortly after death spirits disengages from the physical life to heal from whatever ailed them in life physically, emotionally and mentally. If not please read the answer as well as Chapter 4, Afterlife.

Your mother very well might have stayed with you for a period of time after her death (perhaps the first four or five years), but I don't think your mother continues to be in your life as you say she is, especially not so long after her death nor do I think you would want her to. The process of being finished from this earthly existence is so one can continue achieving spiritual transformation, which will not occur with a continual connection with the living. I do think we can be given assistance and comfort from our dead, but only for a period of time as I previously addressed.

Helpful spirits are usually referred to as angels or guardian angels and/or spiritual guardians, and teachers. These spirits have chosen to be of service to one or more beings on Earth. Their mission and purpose is to bring comfort to those suffering in body, mind and spirit in order the person evolves spiritually. They help to enlighten humanity, person by person. Often times they need "hosts"—living people to act and speak for them.

Many years ago, I met a new friend, an elderly woman who was alone with no family. We met at a checkout counter of a grocery store. She asked the clerk to call her a taxi. Being right behind her I offered my service, "Why spend money on a taxi while I can drive you?" and willingly showed the clerk my driver's license. Barbara, her name, agreed. She was a lovely, quiet woman who had suffered years at the hands of an abusive husband, who had died previous to us meeting. Barbara had broken her back and was limited in getting around. I helped with small things, shopping, cleaning, and once corrected a costly water bill due to a leak. We'd have tea and she'd tell me about her life. She loved my dog and visits from my young son. She called me her angel. Now, I am NO angel! Just a person who met a new friend I really liked. When she passed away only my dog and myself were with her. Afterwards, I followed her exact instructions how she wanted to be buried. Barbara was a gift to me, a sweet friend. How did this happen? I believe her angel planned it out for me to be at the grocery at the right time because a lovely, sick human being needed help.

These are a few ways an angel spirit earns her or his *feathers for her/his angel wings* Your mother very well can be earning feathers for her angel wings, but most likely with another. You might wonder why not you? Really helping a person evolve tough love is often required. That is not easy to do when there is a strong love bond like a mother has with a child. Angels and spiritual teachers are not to fix our problems, rather they are to guide us to make the necessary changes and decisions, which teaches us life lessons.

My suggestion to you is to let your mother focus on her spiritual evolution without you. Yes, continue to say, Hi Mom, I love you, but know she cannot continue to exist in your world with your life issues, challenges and problems. Therefore, I ask you when will you let your mother move on?

I suggest you do a separation blessing ritual. Find a time and space where you will not be interrupted. Create an altar, simple or elaborate––a tabletop or an overturned box with a nice covering. On the altar place a white candle, a fireproof container i.e. ashtray, matches, paper, pen and a photograph of your mother and maybe one of you and her together. It doesn't have to be the original photo because you are going to burn it. You can add other special Mom objects on your altar as well as extra colored candles, flowers and if you like, burn incense.

Light the candle and enjoy the photographs. After quieting yourself, write your mother a thank you letter for what she gave and taught you in life that you hold of value. Tell her how well you are doing with her gifts. Please refrain from asking for her help. You might want to let her know that you are ready to go through this life on your own now because she prepared you so well. Also include your well wishes for her on her spiritual journey. You might want to include how you believe (if you do) that you and she will meet up again when your time comes to cross over.

When the letter is complete light it from the candle and place it in the fireproof container to burn completely and carefully. Now, burn the photograph(s) while expressing something like this, "Thank you, Mom, for all you gave me. I release you to travel your karmic journey as I take another path to my own." If you wish, end your ceremony with, "So Mote it be," which is similar to saying, "This is the truth."

When everything has burned out, snuff out the candle and in your own time put the ashes in a moving body of water or bury in the earth.

• *I attended a séance where you sat as the medium. You spoke about us meeting our loved ones on the other side and when our time has come and we are dying, our loved ones will be with us to help us cross over to the spirit world or heaven, but I wonder what if they have already reincarnated and are no longer on the other side to greet you?* Most likely those who have passed before you will not have reincarnated before you die, and will greet you as you "step over". People who have had a NDE often talk about seeing a relative in spirit holding out a helping hand as though to welcome him or her to the other side. But, if no one you knew in your lifetime greets you then your guardian angel will be your guide. It could be one maybe two of your loved ones have incarnated (come into flesh) before your transition from a physical life to spirit. It is up to the spirit to decide when and where to reincarnate. In my spiritual studies of the Rosicrucian teachings I've read spirits stay on the other side for approximately one hundred and fifty years before they are ready to begin the reincarnation process. Supposedly, one hundred and fifty years is the age we are to be able to live in order life lessons to become whole can be fulfilled. But since it's not necessary set in stone how long we stay in spirit, some return earlier.

If the other side, Heaven or Nirvana or whatever name you give the space, is as lovely as I witnessed and has been described by others, who'd want to rush back?

There is a growing interest of the belief in past lives or reincarnation and karma. This belief has survived through many cultural changes and religions. Even well-known people, from writers and poets to soldiers and leaders of nations, believed that they have lived in different physical bodies and countries. Poets Walt Whitman, Alfred Tennyson and William Yeats all referred to other lives in their poetry. Inventors Thomas Edison and Henry Ford had several conversations about past lives. Plato and General George Patton believed in reincarnation. In Mark Twain's *My Platonic Sweetheart* he refers to a past life in his reference to a girl he had loved in many different lands at different times.

Of the many people over history that believed in reincarnation was the inventor Alan Matheison Turing, who is thought to be the father of theoretical computer science and artificial intelligence. His Turing machine is considered a model for a general purpose computer. Turing was a logical thinking man, mathematician and a theoretical biologist. The movie The Imitation Game betrays his ingenuity in helping Britain win WWII. Turing wasn't considered a spiritualist, or a metaphysician, although he was quoted to have said about reincarnation, "Personally, I believe that spirit is really eternally connected with matter but certainly not by the same kind of body...as regards the actual connection between spirit and body I consider that the body (can) hold on to a 'spirit', whilst the body is alive and awake the two are firmly connected. When the body is asleep I cannot guess what happens but when the body dies, the 'mechanism' of the body, holding the spirit is gone and the spirit finds a new body sooner or later, perhaps immediately."

My point in mentioning famous poets, inventors, men of science and a man of war, is to show the different types of people who believed in reincarnation as a probability.

So again, do not fret if those who loved and knew you and that went before you don't greet you as you take your last breath, you will make the transition.

• *What about people who feel a spirit is present but can't see or hear them?* Sensing or feeling spirit and ghost energy is more common than seeing and hearing them. When we feel the presence of something different from what we physically see or hear in a space or hear we are using what is called clairsentience or clear feeling. A person who can do this is called a clairsentient or psychic empathic. This person is in tune with others' unspoken emotional state or feelings and the vibrations surrounding a person, place or thing. Clairsentients have strong gut instincts or feel like they just know things. Being a psychic empathic is usually more difficult emotionally and physically than being a clairvoyant (the ability to see psychically clearly) or clairaudient (clear hearing). Clairsentients are very sensitive and their nervous systems are too often strained from picking up the feelings of others. It is also more difficult for a psychic empathic to communicate an experience especially with the presence of a nonphysical energy. It is easier to describe when one sees and hears, on the psychic or nonphysical level, a spirit or ghost. See more about ESP abilities in Chapter 12.

• *Why do we have to go to a psychic medium and/or a séance to talk to dead people?* You don't actually have to go to someone to speak to the dead. Communicating with spirits occurs spontaneously at any time, in any place, and to anyone. When clients tell me of their ghostly encounters and spirit experiences, and ask if it could really have been their dead person talking to them, I check my psychic impressions to see if I am in contact with their dead person. Then I can validate, expound and/or give new messages I might receive from the spirit in question or another. Chapter 8, Solo, will guide you in ways to communicate on your own which, in my opinion, is the absolutely best way with the dead.

• *My teen daughter is very interested in communicating with spirits. Is it wise to let her go to a séance with me?* Read my thoughts in previous responses about young people and spirit communication. I wouldn't encourage people under eighteen to take part in a séance. They "spook" too easily, are highly emotional and quite imaginative. Not that the same can't happen with adults. The most important reason is young people can attract pesky spirits––like poltergeists. Children can and do see spirits and ghosts more easily than most adults. I have a grandson, eight years old at the time of publication showing signs for being a gifted psychic with a strong tendency toward spirit communication. I advised him, "If you're going to continue to communicate with the dead you mustn't be frightened by them" as he is at times. We work together to understand the different energies and spirits and how to manage the types of communication he is age ready to experience. His is a rare situation with a grandmother who can guide.

Without knowing your daughter, I would recommend a private session with a reputable medium, but not a séance at this time.

• *At a séance the medium gave me a message from a spirit. When I told her the person wasn't in spirit but still living she said that happens sometimes. Why does it happen?* The person is thinking of you and those thoughts are telepathically strong. Telepathic thoughts occur often, sometimes every day. They are as simple as having a feeling or thought of a person who contacts you within a short time. The communication we have with spirits is telepathic, which means shared thoughts without the usual means of physical communication. If, during a psychic reading or spirit communication, the medium picks up a person who is alive perhaps you should contact that person to find out if she or he is also thinking about you. The person might be in need and you are the one to give a helping hand.

• *How do I clear my home of ghosts or unwanted spirits?* According to various cultures and religions there are several ways to clear away ghosts and other unseen entities. For hundreds of years, Native Americans have used smudge sticks made from herbs like sage or sweet grass for purification ceremonies. If you have no knowledge passed down from family, culture or religious beliefs begin with incense to purify and cleanse your space. Some incense to use would be sage, rosemary, myrrh, frankincense, and sandalwood. I have also used rose and orange blossom. Along with the incense, you can sprinkle rose or holy water around areas you sense negative energy and/or entities. You can buy holy water at a Catholic Church. Rose water along with incense, candles etc. can be found in metaphysical bookstores or occult stores.

Feng Shui, which translates to wind-water, is a Chinese philosophical system of harmonizing with the surrounding environment. The practice cleanses buildings of negative and/or evil spirits and restores balance and beauty to places like homes, places of business, and or graveyards. Feng Shui advises one to hang bells or chimes on the door to keep bad energies out of a room. Every time the door opens to the room the noise will frighten the spirits and chase them away.

• *How can spirits move objects or their footsteps be heard if they are not in body?* It's not easy, or common, to manifest enough energy to move an object, but some spirits can do it. Moving things around is usually ghost energy since they are more attached to the physical world. A niece clearly had a spirit in her bedroom. She would find some small objects on her dresser rearranged. It only happened when my niece was out of the room. We were able to pick-up the woman spirit moving things around. The spirit had no intention of communicating with us and the moving of things happened so rare, we all just let it rest. Spirits/ghosts can also make sounds, like footsteps or creaking doors. Once in a while a spirit will leave a gift, like a coin. It's a message to the living they are making contact. The question below answers more about the meaning of coins and the dead.

• *When I find a penny on the ground or somewhere where I didn't see it before, I've heard it's a signal my dead loved one is remembering me. Do you believe in the penny message?* I do because it has happened to me quite a few times, often in fact. Like you, I've seen a penny where I absolutely know was not there before. Now, I also find dimes. I guess the cost of living has gone up in Heaven also or perhaps a spirit is sending a different message.

A connection between coins and the dead is found throughout history. In ancient Greece an obolus (coin) was placed under the tongue of the dead to pay the fare required by Charon, the ferryman of Hades (the god of the Underworld.) He would ferry the deceased across the rivers Styx and Acheron and into the underworld rather than leave the soul to wander the shore for a hundred years. In Persia, England and the U.S. pennies were routinely placed on the closed eyes of the dead, yet the purpose for this practice is not clear. Some say it was to keep the eyes of the corpse from flying open. In America, visitors might leave a coin on the headstone or at the gravesite of a person who served in the military. It lets the family of the deceased know someone has visited the grave to pay respect. A penny means simply you visited. A nickel signifies you and the deceased trained at boot camp together. If you served with the person in some capacity, you leave a dime. A quarter has a significant message; it means you were with the deceased when he or she was killed. Some Vietnam veterans leave coins as a "down payment" to buy their fallen comrades a beer or for a hand of cards when they are finally reunited.

Knowing the meaning of coins, perhaps you can think of an unexpected penny as a simple "hello" from a spirit, a nickel might remind you of a time when you shared a learning experience, and a dime signifies you went through important life events together.

It doesn't have to be a coin as one person shared in a recent 2017 Dear Abbey advise column. A woman wrote about a special object she and her loving grandmother enjoyed and shared––sand dollars. Her grandmother sent the woman "dollar" postcards and after the death of her grandmother the woman inherited a gold sand dollar necklace that the grandmother wore often. Some time after the grandmother's death, the woman, looking for a new home, found one lone object in a completely empty house–– a sand dollar. She interpreted that as a sign from her grandmother, felt blessed and comforted and purchased the house.

Abbey responded in part that some people believe sand dollars are "coins" scattered by mermaids.

You might also realize a spirit connection through a particular object you and your departed loved one shared that appears out of nowhere at odd times and places.

• *How can I help my spirit communications become stronger?* Communication with spirits is really quite easy if the spirit is willing. Our departed loved ones try to make it easy for us to hear from them. Often they show up in dreams so as not to frighten us and because our minds are free of waking distractions.

We are in an altered state of consciousness when physically relaxed as when sleeping, daydreaming or meditating. In these states we are much more open to seeing and hearing them without questioning the validity of the communication. The most effective way to begin to hear and see on the nonphysical level is to learn to quiet your mind.

You can learn how to communicate with spirits while awake and strengthen your skills by preparing to hear the messages of the spirits and ghosts through first going into a relaxed state. Some easy ways are discussed in Chapter 7, Séances and Chapter 8, Solo. How to improve your ESP skills continues in the answer below.

• *How do I develop psychic/mediumship abilities?* Develop your psychic and medium abilities as you would anything you wish to master by studying and practicing consistently. Please understand that you can have strong psychic abilities but this does not necessarily mean you will talk to the dead. For instance you might have an innate sense of the meaning to dreams or see auras around people and other living things. It might be you can tell the history of an object by holding it or see events unfold in the future. Not all psychics are interested in, or have an ability to talk to the dead.

The first thing you want to do to heighten your psychic abilities is take time each day to quiet your mind and relax your body. This is an invaluable practice to master. Not only will you clear your mind from too many thoughts to receive and send psychic messages, but also your whole life will be healthier and peaceful. When I taught ESP (extra sensory perception) classes, students played fun psychic games. The students would begin with easy tasks like drawing and coloring shapes already chosen by me. After I drew the shape and decided upon the color, I would mentally send my image to the students. As they mentally received my images and colors they'd put them on paper. You'd be surprised how accurate their drawings were!

I suggest you play it with some friends. You can play daily games such as, when the telephone rings and before you pick it up, decide who it is calling. Just let an immediate image or name come to mind. Now answer your call.

Another easy game is to stand in front of a bank of elevators and decide which will arrive first and stand in front of it ready to board. Some outcomes will be better than others. That's okay. Even we psychics/mediums have better days than others. My quiz at the end of the book will give insight into your ESP skills along with suggestions on how to heighten your psychic abilities.

• *Are there times when you meditate on a client's question and there is simply no answer presenting itself?* This has happened and I'm very forthright with the client. Sometimes, when I tell a client I'm unclear, she or he will ask me to go ahead and say what I am receiving. If the client relates to the information, we continue. If I can't receive any psychic information I do not continue the session.

I'm sure your next question is, why does this happen? I no longer search for the answer to this. It just does. Maybe I wasn't the right medium for the person. Maybe it was the wrong day. Maybe the person was not ready for insights. Or, I'm not the right channel for the spirit wanting to communicate. I accept it just is.

• *I've read you have worked with law enforcement on cases involving persons and murdered victims, but what about a suspicious death that appeared to the relatives to not be an accident or suicide?* It is very heartbreaking when relatives search for answers beyond what the police and medical examiner conclude. I always wonder if my connection to their loved one could make a difference. In most cases, it has.

In the case of a lovely young couple whose ten year-old son had expired suddenly, Sally and Jack (not their real names) came with photographs, doctor records and heavy hearts. They were sure the doctors gave their son, Jordon, the wrong medicine causing him to die in the middle of the night. In the session, I saw Jordan with an uncle named Jack who looked a lot like the boy's father. The couple confirmed Jordan's father was named after this uncle who died unexpectedly at twenty-one. I told them Jordon was laughing, happy to be with Uncle Jack.

Sally said Jordan was a giggly, happy boy. The session went on with the parents, at first unable to accept what Uncle Jack and Jordan said. His death was heart failure from an undetected weak heart like his uncle had died from.

I asked the parents a question from something Jordan told me. Did Jordan appear quite tired the week before his death? Was he having difficulty breathing or short of breath? Yes, the parents said. They thought it was his allergies or a cold and they never thought to take him to a doctor. As heartbreaking as it was to learn Jordon's symptoms were to become fatal, they now had an answer.

We met one more time for further communication into Jordan's illness and his thoughts about it. By the second time, they came to a greater acceptance of Jordan's death by natural causes. He asked me to tell his parents not to feel guilty because it was his time to "go home to God." Because they were very religious people, they finally acknowledged their son's death as God's will. No police were involved, no doctors sued. The little boy's laughter rings in my ears today.

• *Is it possible to contact anyone who has passed away or does it depend on the level of spirituality the person had while they were still alive?* It is not the will or necessarily the psychic ability of the medium to communicate with *all* spirits. Some spirits are not interested in communicating with the living just as they might not be willing to communicate with a particular medium. The spirit did not have to live a spiritual or religious life on their earth to come across easily. Some spiritually advanced people more readily choose not to communicate. They fulfilled their karma, understood the earthly life purpose and willingly left the planet to become whole, or elevated to a spiritual plane of love, light, peace and joy. Then again, there was this one reluctant spirit I found most amusing. This spirit said, "Well isn't this interesting that I, a non-believer, find myself in this séance?" The living person who asked for him laughed and confirmed her uncle was indeed skeptic of anything psychic.

• *Do the spirits ever come and seek you out, rather than just wait for clients to come and ask about them?* Spirits have sought, or visited me to be more accurate, to pass on messages to their living relatives and friends. Whenever possible and if the person is willing, I do relate the message. I have learned to not feel responsible or frustrated when

• *For how long will the spirits of our departed loved ones visit?* Although some spirits visit for a short time, perhaps only to show their face or to greet loved ones many years after their deaths, after several years most will not come to communicate as often. There is a sense they fade away and in fact this is what happens with the passing of time. Their connection to the earth and relationships they had when alive are not a priority or interest. This doesn't mean they don't love those they left behind. It means they are busy learning about how to be a better person, filled with wisdom and love. From what spirits have told me, they have jobs or work on the other side also.

• *A watchman was hanging out in the alley in your video (The Haunted Bay SF and Beyond: Walk with a Medium Part One and Two, Youtube.com, why do some spirits travel/visit and others stay put?* (This refers to my San Francisco Bay Area ghost walks and haunts with producer, Ying Liu, as seen on Youtube Part One.)

The watchman must have liked his time in that alleyway. I sensed he had good memories of the many characters walking by him over the years. He comes with the territory so to speak. Perhaps, as I said before, not all energies leave this realm. Staying earthbound didn't seem to be a problem for him. We the living don't have all the answers for the spirit world. The watchman appears again in The Haunted Bay: Walk With a Medium Part Two in San Francisco's infamous Barbary Coast area.

• *Have you ever given incorrect information about a spirit? And if so, what do you do to correct it?* I have given incorrect information. This is why I ask my clients to know as much as possible about the spirit. Then, we can validate what I receive is from the spirit in question. If the information doesn't make sense to the client, I still deliver the message. Its significance might come to the person later. If it is during a séance, it might be meant for someone else in attendance. I always told clients, not all spirits will talk because you ask, and not all spirits will talk through me. If we attempt to contact the spirit and my information is not familiar to the client, I say, "Sorry, that's all I'm getting at this time."

For private psychic readings, clients whose sole purpose was to contact the dead were warned it might not happen. Séance attendees were told not all would get a message or the message they hope for and not all spirits would come through (more in Chapter 7, Séances.) Still, I hope for the best. To correct any error, I could only say I was deeply sorry if the information caused pain, more grief and sorrow.

The most important and painful misinformation from a spirit occurred during my first case with the police. It was the murder of a woman in her home, which went unsolved for many years. Over the period of a few nights, I had a series of dreams in which I was more than a witness—I was the victim of murder. The terror was heart stopping! During the first dream, I literally saw, heard and felt the attack on the woman. At the front door, a hooded, masked killer all in black and gloved pushed his way into the house. The woman fought back vigorously as he bludgeoned her to death. I saw the steel rod in his hand go up and down repeatedly. Helpless to stop it, I writhed in pain and fear as her chilling screams rang sharply in my head.

Immediately upon awakening, I wrote down every piece of information I could remember. I described the rooms she ran into, the furniture she scrambled over and dodged around hoping to escape the assailant. She finally fell beneath his blows. The house was still except for his jagged breathing. With this I awoke, sickened and confused as to why I had this horrific dream. I rarely had a bad dream, let alone a nightmare.

The next night, I was back in the room where the woman lay on the carpet beaten and bloody. She pulled herself up from the floor, slipping on blood and ever so slowly crawled up the stairs to a landing. There she entered through a closed door into a bedroom. A young girl cowered in bed. Her dark hair and eyes were just like the woman's. Together they embraced on the bed: the mother trying to comfort her young daughter. The woman did not die right away. Once again, quietness came and the dream faded away. I awoke with a great sadness and recorded my dream. On the third night, I returned to the house. The woman was whole, not injured. We were in the room where she had fallen. She told me her name and also named a friend of mine. Then she showed me a photograph of a man. This is he, I heard her say. I took note of his looks and when I awoke, once again, wrote the details down.

The day after, I visited the friend of the woman named to share my dreams and notes. The other woman named in the dream was the sister of the murdered woman. My friend confirmed the woman had been murdered. She died in her daughter's bed and the girl had called 911. Within hours, the dead woman's sister further confirmed how she was killed, the details of the house, and her sister's hair coloring, build, age and even the clothes she wore at the time of the murder. Everything was accurate. The following night, the murdered woman visited me again. Gone were the panic and pain. Angrily, she pointed to the same photograph of the man. Again, I wrote everything down focusing on the man. I gave it to the woman's sister details about the man, the dead woman's anger and her great sorrow at the separation from her daughter. In time, her sister showed me a photo of the husband. I confirmed it was he.

The woman had been in an acrimonious divorce with an on-going custody and property battle. The police had looked at the husband, but they never gathered enough evidence to charge him. Since there had been night break-ins in the woman's neighborhood, the police also looked into the possibility of a robber, but since she was home, he attacked her. Unfortunately they had no evidence to charge anyone. There was a lot of anger and bitterness between the families, which was never resolved. The husband forbade the maternal relatives from seeing the daughter until she was an adult. Many years later, a man in prison for home invasion and assault confessed he broke into the house to rob it and consequently murdered the woman when she confronted him. When I heard this from the sister, I was very upset about giving her wrong information. The sister assured me her murdered sister was pointing the finger at the man she feared most, her husband. He had physically and emotionally abused her throughout their marriage. This influenced my psychic impressions. Perhaps the murdered woman believed her estranged husband was behind the killing.

Many, many years later, I apologized to the sister for any harm I did her and the family. Still, the mistake made me aware spirits can, and do give misleading misinformation. What could I do? I could only relate what was shown to me by the spirit. To the best of your ability, check the facts.

• *How do you handle spirits who want revenge on a living person?* I haven't had many dealings with vengeful spirits or ghosts. The closest experience would be the example in the answer above where the woman pointed to her ex-husband as her killer. Implicating him in her murder could have been her revenge for the many years of physical and emotional abuse she suffered at his hands. Certainly, the police investigating the murder put him under a lot of scrutiny. With regards to revenge, I am more liable to go along with the belief as said in the Bible, Romans 12:19-21, "It is mine to avenge; I will repay, says the Lord." My experience with the dead is their desire for restitution, not revenge. When I hear about that situation, I let them know their grievances are heard.

My latest ghost hunt with The Haunted Bay & Beyond Paranormal Investigators was at the Sharpsteen Museum in Calistoga, California. Spirit activity had been recorded on their security cameras. This was sent to me before my visit. The film showed chairs and a table moving across a room along with numerous white globs of flashing lights. I contacted the producer of the paranormal investigation films. She was very interested in finding out more. Before I agreed to ghost hunt this site, I asked not to be given any further information about any activity or ghost sightings in the museum.

When I was in the building, I encountered two female ghosts dressed in clothing from the 1800's. One fumed about an unjust situation, which occurred when she was alive and living in Calistoga. She glared and pointed with an accusatory finger. I followed her steely glare to see materialize a panel of men sitting at a long table, dressed in the same period clothing, facing the woman. She told me they cheated her out of money. The woman gave me her name, Emma, which I then gave to the museum's staff member along with a description of the ghost. The staff member said others had seen the ghost. During our communication the ghost demanded restitution for being swindled out of her invention. She wanted to be historically acknowledged for her creation. A well-known and very successful company was named as the culprit.

After the filming, research proved to have very startling results––she was speaking the truth! Later in a discussion with the museum staff I would learn the woman was Emma Eels who started a women owned company named Callustro around 1885 and which later was stolen (taken over) through shenanigans by several "lying" men as Eels reported.

I let the ghost know she was heard and validated, which helped her be at peace. The work to vindicate her historically isn't over yet. Using the information, I'll encourage the museum staff to include her story in their literature. Perhaps there are living relatives who will take up her cause. Hopefully someday it will be added to an informational source like Wikipedia. She is a most interesting woman, an entrepreneur before her time and certainly as strong willed in spirit as she must have been in life.

As I said before, I like facts! And the Calistoga ghost investigation surely was one of the most exciting documented ghost hunts I've engaged in. Kathryn Bazzoli, board member of the museum, has confirmed ninety percent of the information I received as historical fact both of the museum and another location a block away.

Several months after The Haunted Bay's paranormal investigation Kathryn emailed me with a couple of recent ghost incidents. In it she said, "This is not the first time similar occurrences have taken place."

Her first update was about four women visitors to the museum. Kathryn stayed at the front counter while the women toured the museum walking out of her sight. Suddenly, she heard a loud yelling from the back of the museum in an area where a vintage cottage is attached to the building "Oh my God! Who are these people?" One of the women came running to the front desk demanding to know, "Who is that woman and those men? What do they want?" Kathryn assured her the museum staff was well aware of the ghosts' presence and all was really OK.

A few weeks after that incident, Kathryn, once again at the front counter with a visitor, heard a loud banging from the cottage area. She went to check what or who was making the racket; no one but those two were in the museum. The noise seemed to come from the cottage but no one was there. She went outside, looked up to the roof––no one up there, she went around and near the museum––no one was making any loud noises. Returning to the front desk she shared her findings with the visitor who calmly replied, "You have spirits don't you? I felt them in the cottage. Somebody is mad about something." I believe she was referring to Emma, don't you?

The target release date for the Youtube video for this ghost hunt is scheduled for early 2017. Because of the validity of the historical facts Kathryn and I have considered writing a book about this fascinating rough and tumble Northern California history.

• *Are you a walk-in, and if so, is that how you became a medium?* The first time I was asked if I was a walk-in was in the early 1980's. My reply was "I don't know." I really didn't know much about walk-ins then. Let's first clarify what a walk-in is considered.

In 1979 Ruth Montgomery, psychic and author of several books introduced in her book, *Strangers Among Us,* the concept of what is considered a walk-in. "Walk-ins," she said, "are people from other dimensions who have walked in or came into a mature person's body with the full consent of the person's soul intellect." She also said, "this isn't a forced incarnation or takeover of a body as in being possessed. (I discuss more about possession in a later question). The person agrees to leave her or his body and make it available to this new soul rather than go through physical death.

A walk-in occurrence may take place during a traumatic event like a serious illness or an accident. The situation may include a NDE, but not necessarily so. The person might choose to be open to a walk-in because they never quite fit in, feel foreign in their body, and no matter how they might try, can't relate to anyone. It becomes too painful to continue to try and the person falls into depression. A person who lives this kind of painful mental, emotional and physical life leaves their bodies open to walk-ins. The pain can lead to a depression so severe a person attempts to take his/her life. It is reported that Dr. Martin Luther King, Jr., one of the charismatic civil rights leaders circa 1960, at the age of twelve tried to commit suicide when his grandmother passed away suddenly. At the time of this event, Martin disobeyed his parents' instructions to stay home and not attend a parade. He went and returned hours later to learn his grandmother had died. Grieved from her death and guilty he had disobeyed his parents' orders young Martin went upstairs and jumped from the second story window of his house. Of course he survived to go on and became a historical figure that greatly influenced millions and reshaped American society.

Could his moment of grave despair be considered an opportunity for a walk-in to appear?

Please note: Not all with the above mentioned ills and challenges are open to walk-ins. You will read later my thoughts on my own experience with regards to my NDE and life thereafter.

For those who believe in, and follow the belief of reincarnation and karma, understand we are born to complete a purpose or mission to advance our spirituality by becoming more loving, compassionate and peaceful beings. The mission of walk-ins is to lead humanity into an astonishing new age. They are high-minded entities permitted by another higher spiritual source to take over the bodies of human beings.

What happens after the walk-in has adopted the body and mind? After a period of time and recovery from the trauma or illness, the person usually has noticeable different behavior and her or his viewpoints of life changes. In some religions this might be considered having *found God*. The transition certainly won't be an easy one for many reasons. Family and friends might feel bewildered by the sudden change and think or say such things as "she's not her usual self" or "he seems to have gone off the deep end since the accident" and so forth.

Montgomery says in her book even some walk-ins are so confused and averse to living on earth he or she thinks, "Let me out of here!" Only, the new being has a clear intention and purpose. In time the being will settle down to help humanity advance in intelligent awareness and show them how to take greater care of fellow humans, animals and nature. This certainly sounds like Edgar Cayce who might have been a walk-in. Cayce was an American mystic who is considered the father of the New Age movement. At about the age of thirteen he got struck on the base of the spine by a ball in a school game. After the accident there seemed to be no apparent injury, although he behaved badly. The normally quiet boy threw things at his sisters and was disrespectful to his father. Eventually when put to bed and when asleep he began to talk. As his parents listened young Cayce diagnosed his ailment saying he was in shock. He gave the cure, which his family prepared and applied while the boy slept.

The next morning he remembered nothing of the day, or talking in his sleep. He was back to normal. Soon after recovering he began to have psychic insights for others. In the years following the incident, Cayce, a devout fundamentalist Christian, was unsure whether his gift came from God or the devil or why it was given to him. He didn't sway from his psychic medical readings and over the course of twenty-two years gave thousands of them while also helping advance the acceptance of psychic abilities.

Was Edgar Cayce a walk-in or did the accident open up a part of the brain to give him these abilities? I'll talk more about my thoughts on that later in the question.

The walk-in doesn't defeat her or his purpose by destroying the adopted body. Rather the being continues to care for it, and in some instances, will take greater care of it than the person inhabiting it had before. Food choices often change; the walk-in might become very sensitive to certain foods and become a vegetarian. The person most likely will become interested in, or more devoted to a spiritual practice. To learn more about walk-ins this website is a good quickie learning resource, www.spiritualhealing-now.com/walk-ins.html

The way walk-ins are introduced into a body may be changing. According to Lee Carroll and Jan Tober's 1991 book, The

Indigo Children: The New Kids Have Arrived, these highly evolved beings enter, not only adult bodies, but also infants at the time of birth. Their book describes the children's behavior and how parents can best guide them to fulfill important roles in society. A review of this book by P. Randall Cohan gives some ways to spot Indigo children: "They come into the world with a feeling of deserving to be here, self-worth is not a big issue, they get frustrated with systems that don't require creative thought, school is often difficult for them and they can seem antisocial. If your little angel/devil fits this pattern and you are pulling your hair out trying to relate, you may want to read this book before resorting to Ritalin."

In 2002 Meg Losey, PhD included more terms about these special children in her book, *The Children of Now: Crystalline Children, Indigo Children, Star Kids, Angels on Earth, and the Phenomenon of Transitional Children.* "... a groundbreaking work that shows that a large number of kids come into the world bearing inherent gifts that are beyond strange; they are telepathic, understand subtle energies, and/or have amazing psychic abilities. Many doctors mislabel them as autistic, ADD, ADHD, or suggest other behavioral difficulties. More than half the time, these doctors are wrong. The Children of Now are not defective——they are differently functional. The phenomenon is very real, and more and more of these highly evolved children enter our world every day."

You may know a walk-in. You may even be one. If you have experienced a near fatal event and felt quite different afterwards, ask yourself have your views of self, others and/or your life's purpose changed dramatically? Has another aspect of you emerged such as a talent or ability you had not realized before? Is your purpose in life clearer than it was before the event? If so, what do you need to fulfill it? I suggest you seek support from another or others who accept your thoughts and help guide you to share your message in a loving way. Focus on staying physically, mentally and emotionally healthy. If you need to heal from past pain, find a good source to help you with that.

As well as *Strangers Among Us,* I recommend more recently written books on this subject: Karyn Mitchell's *Walk-Ins/Soul Exchange* and Yvonne Perry's *Walk-ins Among Us.* They discuss how the walk-in experience unfolds, the viewpoint of people who believed they are walk-ins as well as reports why these experiences may be occurring more often.

As I have repeatedly said about any paranormal ideas different or new to you, do your own research and observations. Then you decide for yourself if walk-ins or now, the birth of children with advanced spiritual awareness are a true phenomenon that can be a valid part of your own awareness.

Now to address whether I believe I am a walk-in. I don't believe I am, or at least not fully a walk-in. What I do know is, I was still myself after the accident. Only, different in the sense my experience of visiting the other side (or Heaven) had awakened me to believing strongly in an afterlife. Plus my psychic abilities came on strongly. Therefore, I do think during my NDE I agreed to a higher spiritual entity moving into my physical body. I do believe during my stepping over to the other side and then coming back into consciousness to, in some way, help others gain greater insights to their own spirituality. In that sense, I am a partial walk-in. My way to impart spiritual information was giving physic readings, being a mediator (medium) between the living and the dead, and teaching on a smaller scale, not humanity at large. I have been interviewed many times about how my psychic abilities began. Ying, producer of The Haunted Bay: (Ep. 4) - Interview with a Medium interviewed me after a ghost investigation at the Condor Nightclub.

What I do think happened to me to manifest strong psychic abilities was similar to what Jill Bolt Taylor, neuroanatomist and author of *My Stroke of Insight: A Brain Scientist's Personal Journey,* experienced. Bolt Taylor had a massive stroke rendering her incapable of the ability to take care of mind and body functions. After she completely recovered her mind, her brain and body consciousness shifted away from normal, logical reality and found herself "at one with the universe." Previous to her experience becoming public knowledge, I had read how head injuries often open a part of the brain's creative hemisphere not normally engaged, resulting in greater development of ESP abilities. Some years after the accident when I committed to a regular meditation practice, I experienced a broader understanding of how quieting the mind truly gives great insights to the world around us, and beyond.

After the accident, I had an intense craving to understand the paranormal. My talent for psychic readings and communication with spirits happened rather easily. After all, what I had seen on the other side was how easy it is to see and talk to those who left the physical body. I didn't plan on being a psychic medium or a metaphysical teacher. It just evolved as though it was meant to be, including clients and students who found me through word of mouth. Perplexed as to why this was happening, I asked a hypnotist friend to put me in a relaxed state and question me about these changes in my life. A voice, unlike my own, simply answered, "She was available." Following the answer and while still in the hypnotic state I saw myself floating in an opaque mist, with a white light attached from my naval to some source above me. To tell the truth, I was a bit disappointed. I thought I was chosen because of my wonderful personality or intelligence. I sometimes laugh at how simple the answers to our perplexities and the spiritual world truly are.

• *Do your abilities ever interfere with your personal life?* It has at times over the years. When I first discovered my abilities to see dead people and know things about others, dead or alive, I didn't know how or why it was happening. There were family and friends who had difficulty with my abilities because of religious beliefs. Eventually most accepted it, but a couple of skeptics remain. A very few still think I'm going against God's will. Some acquaintances mocked me when I shared it, saying I'm full of it. There are a few who continue to say I'm lying or conning people; so be it. I know what I've experienced. It used to upset me but I've accepted it as who I am and what I was meant to do, as have those who hold me close.

I understand there will always be some people who are negative and fearful of the unknown and have no understanding when it comes to dealing with someone different from what they perceive as "normal."

One group of people that have had difficulty with my psychic abilities has been physicians. When I try to direct my doctors to what is ailing me, they do not respect my knowledge. My last doctor was most open to what I had to say, but still wanted blood tests etc., which was fine with me. When I told him about my psychic abilities he was the first physician who listened, asked questions and showed interest. He asked when I realized I had these abilities and when he learned it was after my accident, said yes a head injury seems to open up a part of the creative side of the brain. He mentioned he would like to return to medical school to specialize. The school he wanted to attend was very competitive and difficult to be accepted into. I told him it was already done. Forgetting I had said that I was happy to hear six months later he was accepted. Those in the healing profession who also have listened to my psychic impressions about my health are my acupuncturists, chiropractors and massage therapist. I do not always receive health information about myself.

My psychic abilities were especially difficult for love partners to accept. For some reason, they felt threatened by what I did. My ability to talk to the dead wasn't appreciated by love partners as well as family and friends. Finally, I met a man, now my husband, who is most fascinated by my abilities and supports my work.

I know I am not alone with understanding and tapping into the power of intuition. Aristotle was quoted to have said, "Intuition is the source of scientific knowledge."

• *Are you finally at peace with your gift, or do you still question why you can communicate with those passed on?* I am at peace with my abilities. I've had the privilege of counseling people from all over the world. I've spoken with numerous spirits and ghosts. There have been times I questioned the validity of spirit communication. But if it is not true, why do I know so much about those who have passed without having met them? During my darkest hours, when a person I loved very much passed away suddenly, I denounced it all! Later with a therapist's help I learned this denial was part of my grief and he assured me indeed there is spirit communication. My purpose is clear. My work with spirits and ghosts is interesting, mostly fun, and certainly rewarding. Albert Einstein concurred, "The intuitive mind is a sacred gift and the rational mind is a faithful servant. We have created a society that honors the servant and has forgotten the gift."

■ ■ ■

2

LAST BREATH

*While I thought that I was learning how
to live, I have been learning how to die.*

— Leonardo da Vinci —

Two of the greatest mysteries of life are the beginning, birth
and death, the ending. Birth is usually a joyous celebration, full
of hope and dreams, whereas death, a sorrowful time. There
remain many unanswered questions about what happens to us
after we die. What is it like after we take our last breath and
our body ceases to function and becomes cold and heavy, void
of our spirit? Do we transcend to another plane of existence or
are we just energy dispersing into the universe? Some believe
there is no afterlife and once laid to rest our body disintegrates
to dust or ash.

A great deal is known about the physical facts of dying
and how the body decays. Beyond the outward and obvious,

our learned scientists and medical people know very little. In The Huffington Post article Life After Death: Examining the Evidence (4/15/12) physicist and author, Victor Stengar said, "…brain function decreases, we lose consciousness, as when under full anesthesia. Why should that be if consciousness resides in an immaterial soul? Brain scans today can locate portions of the brain where different types of thoughts arise, including emotions and religious thoughts. When that part of the brain is destroyed by surgery or injury, those types of thoughts disappear. Let's face it; so-called spirituality is all in the head. It's purely material in nature. You often will hear it said, 'Absence of evidence is not evidence of absence.' This is not true. Absence of evidence is evidence for absence when that evidence should be there. If life after death exists, then evidence should be there. It is not. Life-after-death can be ruled out scientifically beyond a reasonable doubt." [*sic*]

Some scientists believe that psychologist and medical doctor Dr. Moody, the most recognized author on this subject, studies are flawed, logically and empirically. Longtime advocate of scientific skepticisms and critical thinking, and author of several books and essays, Robert Todd Carroll, says of Dr. Moody's research "Whereas Moody believes NDEs are evidence for an afterlife they can be explained by neurochemistry and are the result of a dying, demented or drugged brain." [*sic*] He further said "…what Moody describes as a typical NDE may be due to brain states triggered by cardiac arrest and anesthesia."

Not all medical professionals agree. Dr. Eden Alexander III provides evidence in his book, *Proof of Heaven: A Neurosurgeon's Journey into the Afterlife*. It's a good read for those, like me, who had a NDE and had difficulty expressing what happened, how they felt about it, and the insights about life, which came from it. Doctors and nurses I shared my NED experience with, and some who work with dying patients, told me some of their patients who were within hours of dying spoke of similar visions I had. The patients said they saw a loved one who was already dead extending comforting love, or they spoke of being in a beautiful, peaceful place in nature and/or seeing a brilliant white light which they felt a pull toward. I encourage you to explore through experiments the possibility of communicating with the dead. You can join with others interested, attend an open group séance, and/or attempt to communicate with your loved ones who have passed and/or the relatives of others who are dead. Don't judge the outcome. Share what you believe you have experienced to learn if it has meaning to another.

Since the purpose of science is to expand its knowledge, and if you, like me, have lived long enough to witness scientific findings change over time, I believe in the future, science will be able to provide proof of life after death. It will be revealed once the physical body dies the mental or subconscious mind continues to exist on some plane, on some level. Continued research in understanding and discovery of brain activity and capabilities will provide the proof.

Although, there are no tangible facts there is life after death at this time, unless you have experienced dying and returned to life or encountered a dead person then you know something quite beautiful has taken place. Something often too complicated to express, and certainly something outside of what science or the medial professionals can explain.

In Dr. Moody's interview with Jeffrey Mishlove, Ph.D., and President of the Intuition Network who conducted hundreds of interviews with leading figures in psychology, philosophy, science, health and spirituality Moody said, "I don't mind saying that after talking with over a thousand people who have had these experiences, and having experienced many times some of the really baffling and unusual features of these experiences, it has given me great confidence that there is a life after death. As a matter of fact, I must confess to you in all honesty, I have absolutely no doubt, on the basis of what my patients have told me, that they did get a glimpse of the beyond."

After death and after some time for those who believe in reincarnation the cycle of life begins again with a joyous event––birth.

■ ■ ■

3

HOW THE DEAD STAY ALIVE

The life of the dead is placed in the memory of the living.

— Marcus Tullius Cicero —

When you die, some people think that's it! It's all over. That's all she wrote. It's a done deal. Many more believe in an afterlife, although most are uncertain if it's possible to continue interaction with their loved ones. Our loved ones who are dead are gone, but not forgotten. Memories of them are kept alive through photographs, recurring special events, places shared, and memorabilia. Even for those who don't believe in spirits or are uncertain if somehow, somewhere we live on will talk to their dead: "What do you think about this, honey?" and/ or "(name) I sure wish you were here right now." People often remark that another is like one of the dead relatives and then go on to talk about that relative. These are a few examples of how the dead remain alive in our minds and hearts. Therefore

I say in many ways there is no absolute ending and the spirit of the person really does continue to exist after death. What if you could get answers to the questions you are thinking or meant to ask? What if you wonder, did he (or she) know I cared enough? Was she sad I didn't come to see her more often? If the deceased could hear you, would your sorrow lessen, depression lift, or guilt dissipate? Would your anger at the death of a loved one disappear? If only you could say one more thing, make amends, make right disagreements and share your words of love with the person, then would your mind and emotion be free from the burden of sorrow? If only...

Certainly the questions above are important and answers to them might ease your mind and heart. Still, there are so many uncertainties and questions about death and life after death. There are no guarantees what you read, learned through religion or have heard, are true. Only your personal experiences and what you believe in an afterlife might help ease your heart. I choose to believe not only is there life after death but communication with the dead is possible. I experienced death and the other side. I saw the light. Although guilt is a part of the grief process and your concerns and feelings are valid, this is not beneficial for a peaceful life. Is your mind open to the possibility of communication with the dead?

If you too believe in life after death and ghosts, you are not alone. While skeptics deny the existence of ghosts and spirit communication claiming there's no real evidence, polls and surveys show the public strongly disagrees. A Huffpost poll from 2005 found 45 percent of Americans believe in ghosts or the spirits of the dead and that they can come back in certain places and situations. In the same year, a Gallup poll found roughly three in four Americans professed a belief in at least one paranormal category. Extra-sensory perception topped the list with 41%, just ahead of the 37% who said they "believed in haunted houses." During a CBS 2005 nationwide random telephone survey of 808 adults, when the question if they believed in life after death 78% said yes and "More than one in five Americans said they have seen a ghost themselves, or have felt themselves to be in the presence of one." The survey also reported, "...half of younger Americans aged 18 years to 45 years believed in ghosts with those over 45 less likely." Women were twice as likely as men to say they've seen a ghost "...56 percent of women were more likely to believe in ghosts than 38 percent of men." Generally, I think women tend to be more sensitive than most men to the unspoken emotions and reactions to others around them and therefore, more sensitive to the unseen energy.

The concept of a ghost is based on the ancient idea that a person's spirit exists separately from his or her body, and may continue to exist after the person dies. Because of this many societies used funeral rituals as a way of ensuring the dead person's spirit would not return to "haunt" the living. Zulus burn all of the belongings of the deceased to prevent the evil spirits from even hovering in the vicinity. Some African tribes would set up a ring of fire around the bodies of their dead to singe the wings of the spirits and prevent them from attacking other members of the community. Traditional Roma (also spelled Romany or Romani, can be known as Gypsies) believe if the death of a person is already foreseeable, the fire and light of candles, which have to burn until the funeral, have a purifying power as well as the power to keep away the spirit of the dead. In order to "smother" the spirit of the dead, the Romanian Kalderaš take one piece of soil from the grave of the dead and throw it into a well. Funerals in Western countries, including Christian and Jewish funerals, involve prayers to give comfort to the deceased's family and friends, as well as to ask for a safe passage of the soul into the next world.

Well-known New Zealand anthropologist Raymond Firth, notes that many funeral rites are associated with "ideas of completeness of sequence in human affairs" analogous to farewell ceremonies. Can it be like in life when we say goodbye we anticipate that person we will see the person once again?

No matter what ritual or celebration you perform to honor the deceased do it with sincere feelings for I do believe spirits feel the helping energy as they transition. In time the person will return in spirit to thank you. Remember, although ghost haunting is often not a pleasant encounter, visitations from our dead can be a most comforting experience. Memories remind us to celebrate their time and experiences we shared and to send them heartfelt love when we are thinking of them.

■ ■ ■

4

AFTER LIFE

*And I saw the dead, small and great, stand before God;
and the books were opened: and another book was
opened,
which is (the) book of life: and the dead were judged out of
those things, which were written in the books, according to
their works.*

*— Revelation 20:12 King James Bible "Authorized
Version", Cambridge Edition —*

Worldwide and historically many people have believed
in life after death. Buddhism, Hinduism, Sikhism, Islam,
Zoroastrianism, Judaism, and Christianity all teach there is life
after death. Some of the most influential thinkers of the world,
such as the philosopher Plato, had thoughts about what occurs
after death. He believed logical and critical thinking can attain truth and enlightenment, and suggested it could come in

a mystical experience. In much of his writings (The Republic, Phaedo and Gorgias) Plato discussed how the soul, after being separated from its body, may meet and converse with the departed spirits of others and be guided through the transition from physical life to the next realm by guardian spirits.

The Rosicrucian Order, AMORC, (a community of seekers who study philosophy and metaphysical laws) believes when souls pass through transition they are in various states of consciousness. At death, most people fall into a deep slumber, which enables them to forget much of life's unpleasantness and tensions. Low-grade entities usually retain consciousness and fight to get back into a physical body as soon as they possibly can. The advanced soul proceeds in full consciousness away from the earth and up to the higher realms. The highly developed soul, the conscious Master and the advanced student pass over in full waking consciousness and are usually met by their own Master of a High Being sent by the All Infinite One to minister to them.

Souls present themselves immediately to the Board of Judgment. This is not a judgment in the sense the life is adjudged to be a success or failure and corresponding rewards or punishments meted out. The main intention of this Board is to find a way your soul may be given the greatest possible opportunity to balance out its debt to life and learn how to complete its evolution.

This Board acts at all times for the good of the individual and for the best interest of the entire human evolution. After the soul and the Board have examined the life just passed and assayed how near it came to attaining plans and keeping promises made before birth, a decision is jointly reached. The soul then sets to work at inner levels to expiate as much of its karma as possible in the astral world. There is nothing painful in this. It is a joyful service and fills the soul with a sense of accomplishment.

This Board is composed of at least three and sometimes more, highly developed entities with computer–like minds which assess and evaluate every single thought, emotion and action of the entire life, even the very smallest and most seemingly insignificant. Then, based upon this evaluation, the place, type and duration of future training and instruction for the soul is determined.

Most souls passing from the body are given a "spiritual vacation," a relief from the pressures of life. The average individual is given an opportunity to visit with loved ones who have previously passed for a certain period of time to renew associations and enjoy the happiness, which they have been taught to expect. If relationships were not harmonious on earth or no attempts were made to make the relationship loving and harmonious, then in death the same relationship problems and lack of compassion continue to exist. I suggest you make amends whenever possible, and/or do your best to forgive an offending party. By forgiveness I mean stop mentally going over the act you believe (or did indeed) hurt you in some way; put it to rest unless you want to deal with the same situation and person in the afterlife.

Often people believe when they die they will immediately be ushered in pomp before the throne of God and all people will love them unconditionally. Alas, a person who is morally weak, or evil will see him or herself quite clearly for whom she or he truly is, and will receive just treatment from those they hurt when living. This can mean asking for forgiveness, or agreeing to reincarnate to a life of punishment, that is being treated as they treated others in previous lives.

In spirit we do not stay the same just as we hope we do not in life. In spirit as we heal, gain knowledge, understand and pay off our debts, we transform. As I've said before spirits can appear at younger ages than when they died. It's their choice how they want to be remembered. Our beloved ones want to help their earthly loves be comforted so for a period of time will appear in human form. They can look the same as at or near the time of death or if they chose, at a younger age. Please understand, this isn't how they will be forever.

I learned more about what takes place after the spirit transitions from communicating with my deceased sister than from any book. She died suddenly in 2010 and afterward, I talked to her everyday as I had when she was alive. Sometimes she participated, sometimes not. In the fourth year after her death I called on her by name. She took a couple of days to respond and told me she no longer was known by that name. She didn't tell me what name to call her other than "sister." In late 2015 she awoke me in the early hours of the morning with a message. It was information I never knew about spirit transformation. My sister showed how her entire being as I had known her, that is the physical person I knew, no longer existed. She appeared in my mind as I knew her and then within seconds the physical being began fade away. The physical body separated into energetic cells. It truly was amazing to witness. The cells appeared like sparks of light or little shooting stars. They integrated with all matter in the skies—the entire universe. There was a sense, not words or images, that my sister was everywhere in nature. She had become a part of *The All*. Some might think of this as cosmic energy, universal flow and/or God. It was awe-inspiring. To the very core of my own cells, I experienced the power and vision of *The All Divine*. What my sister expressed through images reminded me of the bereavement poem, "Do Not Stand At My Grave And Weep" by Mary Frye (1931.) In it Ms. Fry asks those grieving her not stand at her gravesite and weep for she is not there, she does not sleep. Further in the poem she writes where her spirit will be found:

> *I am a thousand winds that blow.*
> *I am the diamond glint on snow.*
> *I am the sunlight on ripened grain.*
> *I am the gentle autumn rain.*
> *When you wake in the morning hush,*
> *I am the swift, uplifting rush*
> *Of quiet birds in circling flight.*
> *I am the soft starlight at night.*
> *Do not stand at my grave and weep.*
> *I am not there, I do not sleep.*

My sister also revealed how, after a time, her cells would re-unite to form a new physical body when she incarnated (back into flesh.) Her DNA within this new body would consist of renewed healthier cells while containing memory of past life-times. Her spirit would be prepared to learn new life lessons.

My sister was, as far back as I could remember, devoted to spiritual practices and teachings. She had been an active Catholic, and later a devoted Rosicrucian, Reiki Master, and a student of herbal healing and alchemy. Unfortunately, she suffered from hereditary illnesses and died in her late sixties before she attained a healthier body. She was a very kind, loving person who put the welfare of others before her own needs.

Thankfully, in life and the afterlife she continues the process of transforming her DNA for a healthier future life. I don't doubt her vision of a future incarnation as a healthier person and am sure she shared this information with me so we continue our spiritual practice and knowledge together as when had when she was alive.

The key in life is to see yourself clearly through the eyes of your soul and not another's image of you as good or righteous, bad or worthy. Seek to understand you are myriad of energies that will last long after the physical body ceases to exist. Avoid giving injury to others and yourself with negative thoughts, words or physical actions. Endeavor to live with love and compassion to all living things to the best of your ability. Prepare to be in the best state of health——spiritually, mentally, and physically——when you are released from your physical existence and enter into an etheric one.

■ ■ ■

5

BEFORE TALKING TO THE DEAD

The fear of death follows from the fear of life.
A man who lives fully is prepared to die at any time.

— Mark Twain —

Before you begin spirit communication, decide your purpose. What is it you want to achieve from talking with the dead? Is it to know if they are at peace? Or out of pain? Maybe you need to know if they are still with you. Is it advice you seek? Stop now and reflect on your intentions so you are clear with why you are communicating with spirit. You might want to note your answers so you can come back to them later.

In this chapter you have an opportunity to examine your reasons and expectations from talking with the dead. This allows you after the communication to gauge whether your purpose was satisfied.

Your belief about death, and what happens to your soul or spirit thereafter influences the communication. Interaction with the dead is a personal experience based on religious, spiritual, and cultural background. Religions teach us there is life after death. It is often referred to as eternal life. Many people believe living a decent life will reward them a heavenly place of peaceful rest. For those who have been wicked and evil, hellish torment with no chance of rest awaits them. If you fear what is to come, your communication can attract fearful, unhappy or even confusing messages from the beyond. Those who trust life exists after death will most likely have a clearer and faster response from the dead. If you believe life is a learning experience, forgiveness is achieved through understanding, and redemption is a possibility, most likely your communication with the dead will be full of hope and enlightenment.

Even those with strong religious beliefs can find themselves questioning what happens after the spirit leaves the body and feel uncertain in times of grief about life after death. Although most of us accept dying as a reality of life, when death takes a person or a pet we loved dearly, or anyone with whom our lives are entwined dies, we are often emotionally crushed. Confusion penetrates the mind and challenges our faith about the beautiful aspects of death and what occurs thereafter. In the first stages of shock over a loved one's dying, many question their religious and spiritual beliefs. Great sadness, like a physical illness, can weaken our faith. We cannot seem to move beyond our heavy hearts to hear comfort from those surrounding us, let alone a god. Life seems to be a painful existence.

At my own times of grief even with many years of spirit communication, I have questioned my personal and professional experiences. I've denied what I knew; the ability to speak to the dead exists. Then something happens. A dream so real, I heard her voice plainly, she touched my arm, a blur of fur and my favorite kitty flew past me. She expired a few months ago, I remind myself. Only I see her clearly sitting in the window seat like she always did. I hear my sister call my name. It can't be. I laugh at my imagination. After all, she's been gone for a few years now. She laughs with me. I am comforted by the interaction.

Surprisingly, even if we felt no affection for the person, we experience sadness, and, very often depression from feelings of guilt. We might think we shouldn't have judged the person harshly and we should have been kinder. With a loved one's death, the guilt is even stronger. We think; I should have done more. She (or he) would have lived longer if only I had fixed her health problem, recognized her depression. I should have spoken up, told him I loved him more.

Maybe there was an unresolved disagreement before the person died and now you can't go back and fix what went wrong. Many times someone passes away and leaves the grieving to mentally replay unspoken words, sentiments, and unsolved issues. A loved one's loss can create an enormous emotional unbalance.

One night I was lost when I turned onto a rural road. There were no streetlights and it was very dark. I could barely see ahead of me. Panicked, I started to cry and beg God for help. My father appeared sitting in the car's passenger seat next to me. I was startled at his presence. Not because he'd been dead twenty years, but I hadn't gotten along with him all that well. He pointed in a direction further down the road where I could see some lights to my right. Stubbornly, I refused to acknowledge him. I didn't want his help when he was alive nor did I want to communicate with him in spirit. But then again, he had a great sense of direction, being a very practical man. So, I followed where he pointed. When I made it to a lighted road leading me to my destination, I thanked my father for his help. Since his death he's come to my aid more than once. Separated by death, we are creating a healing between us. Perhaps, like me, you can heal a relationship beyond the physical world. It isn't too late.

Love is powerful. We continue to love our dead. Sometimes we talk about our love of them out loud, but more often it is in our minds, we talk to them. But, do they really hear us? That's the most asked question of me. My answer is, they do. Whether they respond in a timely manner or with the answer we hope for is another thing altogether. More often than hearing them we sense or feel their presence. People have told me they experience familiar scents associated to the dead person when thinking of her or him. This is the spirit making contact with you. He or she may be telling you, "I'm still with you."

Do they really talk to us? When they want to and only if we hear them will they continue to communicate. This is the most difficult part for the living––to hear the conversation of the dead. Let me remind you there is a time when communication with spirit must lessen, or expectations of your loved one continuing to talk with you must cease. This doesn't mean you have to erase all memory of your beloved one or to stop loving them. That'll never work! Rather, stop calling on the spirit to come to fix something or to comfort you at every challenge you meet in life. The spirits must get on with their own transformation. Most likely you will meet again when you cross over, if the spirit hasn't reincarnated, which rarely occurs before your time on earth ceases.

Who would you like to communicate with? Why do you wish to talk to her or him? Be clear whom it is you wish to talk to and hear from. Think of the person's name, write it down then mentally see her or him clearly, maybe even pick out a photograph to look at before and/or during the period of communication.

Do you have a message? What it is you'd like to know or what is it you want to ask? My advice to have a greater chance for positive communication to take place is to keep it short and simple. You may say, "Daddy, no one understands me like you did. The other day Johnny threatened to take away my part of your house. You left it to me in the will! I hate him. He's always bullied me when you aren't around, like now. Why did you have to die? I need you. Tell me what to do with that horrible son of yours."

Can't you just hear Daddy's spirit saying, "Oi, there goes the kids fighting again! I hate to get involved."

If you want your message to get through easily and clearly keep it simple. Here's an example. "Daddy, Johnny and I seem to be at odds again. Any words of loving wisdom for us?"

I, and millions of other people who have experienced grief, empathize with you. But, when in a strong grieving time it hinders clear spirit communication. Will you please wait until you have some kind of control over your emotions?

Be direct with your thoughts. Who do you want to contact? What is it you want to know? Say the name or title of the person, as some mediums ask during a séance. If it's a parent or grandparent, call them what you did when they were alive. Then state your purpose for the communication and your hope for guidance or some form of reply.

Keep emotions, such as blame and pleading, in check or to a minimum. For instance your person may have died in an accident––you think in some way you could have prevented it? You feel guilty? Do you want to know if you are forgiven? Communicating in guilt and sorrow you might say, "God, Barry! It's all my fault you're dead. I should have been more insistent you not leave the house that night. You were too drunk. It was my fault for giving you the liquor. I'm such a screw up. If only I had prevented you from leaving you wouldn't be dead. I miss you so much. Life is not worth living without you. I wish I was dead too."

Poor spirit Barry wanting to adjust in the heavens, burdened by your guilt, sad for your unhappiness. He wants you to know he wasn't paying attention to his health. He takes responsibility for the accident. You are forgiven for any feelings of guilt over his death. Have a good life, he says, and reminds *you* to stop drinking and driving.

Clients come every year to ask about a dead relative or friend I've already contacted and imparted a message. It's a dead subject, I tell them. Some keep asking, "Does she forgive me yet?" "Is he still around me?" The answer is still the same.

Let the spirit you wish to contact rest! Quit calling him back over and over.

The clients, not ready and unable for simple answers went on to suffer for a few more years before finding inner peace and for some, never finding it no matter what the spirit conveyed.

How exhausting emotionally for all involved, the inquirer, the spirit and the medium aware of the turmoil and hoping to present a reasonable communication from spirit to the over-wrought person.

The scenarios above were actual spirit communication in private sessions. They are true statements the living make when enduring the pain of a loved one's death. Don't keep asking the same question.

Can you trust a medium to communicate for you and be-lieve the answer she gives to your pain is the correct one? If not, see a licensed therapist to relieve you of emotional pain.

Please know I'm not unsympathetic. I too have been in deep grief. I too felt the emotional need to keep contact with someone I loved greatly. Perhaps you may find solace for your grief as I did with a grief counselor. After a period of time if you find your grief has your life in shambles, perhaps a thera-pist or psychotherapist can provide a better healing for you than a psychic/medium healing.

Sorrow can keep us from voicing sentiments and thoughts. I suggest you first take time to calm your thoughts and then write down what it is you would like to ask or know from the other side. Here's how you can begin your communica-tion: Like with any form of written communication (and you can do this when speaking also) first give a greeting——"Hello, (write or say the name of the spirit or title as Dad, Mom, dear husband or sweet wife) this is me (give your name.)" Now, ask your question. "George, are you free from the cancer pain?"

A great interest the living has about a loved one who suffered a long illness, and was in terrible pain and discomfort for months before dying, is she or he finally free of all of that? Asking about release of a painful illness at death is reasonable. You most likely will hear from the spirit or medium, "She (or first person, I) finally can breathe easy again." And more often than not, spirits have said to me, "It's great to move around without pain" as they described the location of where the pain they had when alive. Still, the pain a loved one went through can often continue to haunt us, the living. Please, as best you can, stop your own mental and emotional anguish and rest assured that your loved one is out of physical pain. It is true some spirits continue to hold on to their pains—*I suffered so much* they bemoan. Pray for them to find release from their sufferings.

It is very difficult for us, the living, to accept that pain has a spiritual purpose. Many, many times clients have asked me, "Why did (name) have to suffer so long?" and "Why couldn't he or she have died quickly?"

My personal experience was with the passing of my ninety-six-year old mother. She had a stroke, which set her on the course of a four-month process of dying. I called that time the "long good-bye." She had been a most loving, supportive mother in spite of her share of life sufferings. It was in her later years she found a freedom to be happier, thus it pained her family to watch her slowly and painfully diminish physically, and mentally. I searched for why this was happening to her and to us, her children who loved her greatly. She had been a good woman, a devoted Catholic who volunteered with charitable organizations. The only answer I came to accept of her suffering was from my spiritual studies and belief in karma.

In our last few weeks of her life she expressed her fear of dying alone. Was this a carryover from her previous life? When I was studying for my certification in hypnotherapy my interest was past life regression. I recruited family and good friends to practice my skills. Although my mother didn't believe in past lives, she happily went along with the experiment, and went easily into a very relaxed state of hypnosis. With clarity she began to speak of another lifetime as though in the present time. "I'm in bed sick," she said. She gave further details about a life as a young woman with a serious illness confined to bed in an upper room of the house. The majority of time was spent alone with only her father caring for her needs. When she heard him leave the house she would get out of bed to sit at a small window staring out at the world wishing for a healthy life and company. Her long hours of loneliness and fear of death caused much anxiety and depression. Finally death came. She succumbed to death, alone and frightened. In this lifetime my mother suffered from depression, which she endeavored to overcome through medication.

I didn't want my mother to leave this world experiencing the fear of dying alone. I prayed she could take with her how much she was loved and cared for up to that time. When the Hospice nurse told us my mother's death would be any day I decided to do a meditation learned from my Rosicrucian teachings. You might find it helpful when your terminally ill loved one is days or moments away from the end of life, or, as it is intended, when the person has just died. For either, you can do this visualization meditation up to seven days before or after death.

Imagine or envision the person walking toward a brilliant sun. You might visualize the person in a healthy state and dressed in all white, or not. When my sister died I saw her as she appeared at the time of her death. She was walking a path that led to the sun. Each day in my daily meditation she appeared healthier, more energetic, younger, and happier. The light from the sun grew brighter and whiter as she walked closer to it. On the seventh day, she turned toward me, smiled and raised a hand in farewell before she was fully evaporated into the light of the sun. I was sad to say goodbye, but joyful my sister made to the other side to rest in peace and joy.

My vision of my mother was different. I started the meditation the week the nurse alerted us death was soon for her. Once again, I went into a meditative state with the idea I would do as described above, only my mother's spirit changed it. On the first day a sudden image in my mind's eye appeared. I saw Mother as a ten-year-old girl. She was wearing an outfit that I recalled from an old photograph of her, one I hadn't seen for years. Instead of walking to the sun she was in a kitchen being fawned over by her smiling mother and father. She was giggling and hugging her parents. They were obviously very happy to be together once again. It was no secret to the family that my mother, the youngest and only girl of six boys, was a most cherished child. Behind them stood my smiling sister, Mother's eldest child, who died six years previous.

The next day my visualization of my mother was still of the child full of laughter, only now she skipped toward a bright, white light. For two more days I watched her in my meditation skip along the path as that ten-year-old girl, laughing all the while, moving closer to the light. On the fourth day I saw nothing but a gray blank wall. Disturbed, I tried visualizing her as I had been. Finally, I accepted that she, her spirit, had made the transition. Her physical body was still in a coma state.

Two days later my mother took her last breath and was declared physically dead. The Hospice nurse arranged Mother's Rosary beads in her hand. I laid my hands over hers and the Rosary beads to recite her favorite prayer, "Hail Mary, full of grace, the Lord is with thee. Blessed are thou amongst women."

To add to this, as family met at my mother's deathbed, a niece told me she had a dream where "Granny was a kid wearing (described the same outfit in the photo) and was in a bright yellow kitchen with her parents, hugging." Was this a coincidence? Or, did her spirit show us she was happier and ready to leave an old, sick body?

I hope the karmic lesson my mother learned was how very well loved she had been and still is. In this lifetime, my mother's many children, grandchildren and friends surrounded her daily to hold her hand, spoon feed and spice up her life with a bit of gossip and humor as she prepared to transition out of the physical body into the spiritual body.

Medium and Medical Intuitive, Rebecca Conroy-Costello, RN, in her article, Suffering During the Dying Process Has a Purpose, Fate Magazine, Issue No. 729, says our soul and spirit are learning valuable lessons necessary for spiritual advancement. Additionally, she writes that the suffering person is burning karma for some misdeed to others, or that some people who have lived a kind and good life "...have a slower dying process because fear of crossing over."

Some ill people linger and die slowly in a way to comfort those they are leaving behind. The person knows how greatly he/she will be missed and how much he/she will miss being with those he/she is leaving behind. The dying person feels the strong hold of love from those unwilling to accept her/his death and can't break the connection. There certainly can be other reasons, but the bottom line is, suffering can bring spiritual enlightenment. Nevertheless, it is a most difficult, sad experience on both sides.

After my mother's death I suffered guilt, wondering if I made the right decisions for her comfort in the final months. I lamented my impatience with her as she aged. *Did she forgive me?* This was my biggest heartbreaking worry. She comes to me in dreams with a heartfelt feeling of love. A dream I had that really helped heal my troubled mind was one where I was helping her to pack-up for a long trip. She had two large suitcases so stuffed full of clothes I couldn't close them. I said, "Mom, you can't take all this with you." She agreed. "Well, then, June, let's leave what's not needed behind." I knew the message was for me heal the feelings of guilt. She is the same loving, forgiving mother I always knew. After that my memories turn more to our happy times, like listening to her play the piano.

As time goes by, I realize how I have transformed from that painful experience and learned greater empathy. During the long goodbye I developed greater patience, something my mother told me my whole life I needed to learn. During my mother's illness she told me that she needed to express her fears without having anyone offer advice. Now, I listen clearly to others without jumping in to "fix" things. The most important lesson I learned was to never hold back showing gentle love with a kind word and to hold hands and hug often. I am satisfied the time spent with my mother during her death process was used wisely and she had the love needed to face death knowing she wasn't alone.

Maybe you are suffering from guilt and will ask your departed love, *"I'm sorry I didn't come to see you when you were ill"* or *"Are you mad at me?"* This is common to feel and think like this. The majority of spirits do not carry grievances beyond the threshold of death. Why should they? They are free of worldly concerns and issues. They have a higher perspective about human's emotional issues and follies. Perhaps your departed loved one was sad you didn't come when he or she was alive. Maybe she or he wanted to tell you something special. During spirit communication have no doubt, something meaningful to ease your pain will be communicated.

Will you trust when forgiveness is communicated from the other side and know it is time to *forgive yourself*? I hope so and remember keep the happier memories of that special person.

Anger is a normal part of death. People often cry, *"Why did you leave me so unexpectedly?"* and *"How could you leave me?"* If your grief cannot heal hopefully what is communicated to you through spirit, will help soothe your anger at the deceased for dying suddenly. There is a thought of some spiritualists that we die when what we came to earth for is fulfilled. It is not an easy belief to accept or understand when we see children and people who die at the hands of others.

Just because someone dies doesn't mean all is immediately well. One might reflect and inquire with *"I'm sorry I just didn't see you were sad* (or depressed or ill). *Are you happier now?"* If a spirit comes back with, "I'm still very sad," or "I feel lost," don't think peace for the spirit will not be found (although for some few spirits as mentioned before this does happen)! The dead in the other dimension will have to work through issues of depression in order to have understanding of the basis of it. (More in later chapters about what happens after death.) Give your loved one time in the afterworld. Meanwhile, pray that she or he be at peace. A simple, *"I pray* (name), *that you find peace in the afterworld you couldn't find in life."*

You can add an uplifting, cheerful energy in the form of a color such as yellow, green, blue or pink or any pleasant color. Or, send an image of a peaceful setting, a place you might have shared with your loved one. There are so many things we want to know from our dead relatives and friends. Spirits also give us positive words and advise. If they see us suffering they might send simple words, like calmness if we are frantic with life decisions. They might send an image of a quiet place on earth. Maybe a place you and he/she shared, a fun place as a reminder that life still holds good times. Remember, spirit communication is telepathic (more on that later.)

If you decide to talk to the dead on your own, understand your emotions and thoughts do, and will, be jumbled by your grief. I do not encourage you to attempt communication with a spirit right after death. It's just too difficult emotionally to send and receive clear communication. In your grief your longing to reconnect with your loved one might attract another, not so loving, entity to answer your pleas for communication. In the upcoming chapters you will learn how to contact spirits in a safe and loving way. If you insist on contact immediately following the death, I suggest you do it through a trained medium.

If communication doesn't happen spontaneously, or you are uncertain by the response, a medium can be helpful. This is one of the greatest advantages of a medium because she or he isn't connected emotionally to you, the living, or to the spirit in the same way you both had been and are still, attached emotionally. In time you can make contact if your intentions are sincere and your inner ears open.

■ ■ ■

6

SELF PROTECTION

*How can you protect yourself by carrying
a sword if you don't know how to use it?*

— *Terry Pratchett, Author, Monstrous Regiment* —

It's healthier all the way around to educate yourself before speaking with the dead. You do not want to carry around the spirits of the dead or of entities of the unknown in your waking or dream state. This really does happen, especially for the novice, the young, or the fearful. I taught all my students the importance of self-protection both physically and psychically. In other words, *"Don't take it home."* Channeling spirits and other entities is hard on the body and emotions. It is a drain on your energy to open the psyche if not handled properly. Rest, and proper nutrition is needed. A less stressful life adds to the energy needed to be a healthy, happy psychic medium.

Keep close in your soul and thoughts a Divine Being at all times when engaging your psychic energy. Well-known medium, John Edwards prays to Mary, Jesus or God's mother, for an hour before his sessions. Decide which divine spiritual being, whether an angel, spiritual guide and teacher, God, Allah, Buddha, the Goddess, the Master Within, you will connect with during your session. Keep this connection as you go into meditation. Feel the presence guiding and protecting you.

A psychic and medium needs to keep a distance emotionally, physically, and mentally from psychic impressions, messages, images, and spirit presence so not to be affected by them in personal and professional life. Rather, a medium is the observer; seeing, hearing, feeling and knowing from a distance. Before embarking on psychic communication surround yourself with white light. Imagine yourself sitting in a clear white bubble or balloon. It can also be a pastel blue or pink. Mentally clear your space before channeling and receiving psychic information through meditation and prayer, chanting and/or singing. Follow my suggestions and you will make a clearer connection to spirit.

■ ■ ■

7

SÉANCE

And many of them that sleep in the dust
of the earth shall awake, some of everlasting
life, and some to shame and everlasting contempt.

— Daniel 12:2: King James Bible
"Authorized Version", Cambridge Edition —

The most sought after and common way for communicating with the dead is through a medium at a séance, which can be a private one-on-one or group session. Learn more about mediums acting as mediators in Chapter 9.

Séance is French for "seat, session," derived from Old French seoir, "to sit." The American Heritage® Dictionary of the English Language, Fourth Edition says, "The older original French meaning referred to "sit" or "take a seat in a meeting." Perhaps as in a community or political meeting where attendees bored with speakers fell asleep or appeared to be in a trance. It was first recorded in English in 1845. In French, as in English, the word came to be used specifically for a meeting of people to receive spiritualistic messages. Now it means taking a seat where more than one person gathers for the sole purpose of contacting the spirit(s) of the deceased. If a medium is present, she communicates with the spirit and then relays messages from the dead to the living.

Séances can be quite mundane and not as mysterious as most think. For many years, I have been involved with and conducted séances as both a participant and a shared or sole medium. There are usually no peculiar going-ons like knocking, banging on walls, howling dogs, levitating tables and chairs or floating ghosts. There can be a sudden drop in temperature or a cool breeze might move through the room. Sometimes the presence of another person in the room, not included of the original group, can be sensed. On a rare occasion, a white light or a translucent, wispy form may appear and, in an even rarer occurrence, an actual physical image of a dead person may manifest.

You may feel something brush pass you or feel as though someone or something is touching you. The hair on the back of your neck or arms may rise up for no apparent reason. You could hear a voice or sound. You may just *know* you are speaking with a spirit. There are many ways to communicate with spirit energy. There are also as many different spirit energies as there are many different kinds of people.

What I find interesting and enjoy most in séances is how uplifted the participants are when positive messages come from departed loved ones.

The séances I've been involved in range from the more formal seated at a table, holding hands in a semi-darkened room to a lighter, casual sitting around an office or small auditorium with no hand holding. They all included a form of a short introduction of what to expect, quiet time for a meditation, a prayer, and at times, singing. In the séances where I was the medium and after we started, I would announce what spirit had made her/his presence known and with whom the spirit wished to communicate. Sometimes I was incorrect about the participant, but within a moment it was straightened out. Often a name would come through, certainly a physical description even if the spirit came across years younger than the age of death. Sometimes, none of the participants recognized a spirit. Although it didn't happen often, I'd thank the spirit and return to the séance. Alas, not all spirits come through just because you ask for a message. When I tell people this they are surprised and wonder why. I tell them as in life just because you call or email a person doesn't mean they will respond. Perhaps the spirit is in a state of peaceful rest and what you are doing is no longer a concern.

At times, spirits the participants hadn't consciously thought about contacting will appear and make their presence known. This spirit could be a relative such as a long lost cousin or uncle even the participant hadn't met. It could be a grandparent the participant knew only briefly. I've heard from the spirit of neighbors, childhood friends, and a grammar school teacher. At one séance, an Army man appeared to talk to an older gentleman in the group. The gentleman was befuddled.

HOW TO TALK TO SPIRITS 121

He didn't recognize this man at all. Luckily, I heard the man's name clearly and with the information the gentleman lowered his eyes and became still. The Army man was his friend; more like a brother, said the gentleman, in grade school. The Army man moved to another state and they lost touch. The gentleman hadn't known this friend joined the Army, let alone died in Vietnam, which was the information the Army man gave me. Funny thing, said the gentleman, he'd thought of him off and on and wondered how he was doing.

People wonder why spirits come through if there wasn't a connection to the person for a long time, or at all. The answer is simple. They have a message for you, perhaps advice about a particular issue you are dealing with, maybe to remind you of the shared relationship. It could be the spirit is attracted to you because she or he has fond memories and wants to say "*Hello*" or "*I'm thinking of you and sending good thoughts.*"

There have been times I gave a message only to learn the person sending it wasn't dead but alive. As I mentioned before, messages are telepathic and the messenger is either thinking of the receiver or they will connect at a later date. I never dismiss messages nor attempt to decipher them. I'm the channel for messages between senders and receivers.

Pets were also inquired about at séances. Even if they weren't, many times I would psychically see the spirit of a dog, cat or bird moving around the room. If you are interested in, and have yet not read my thoughts about pet spirit communication, please see the eleventh (11th) question *Can pets that have passed away communicate with us?* in Chapter 1. Included in it is a simple ritual for communicating with your deceased pet.

Penelope Smith's *Animals in Spirit* gives examples and suggestions in helping you contact your beloved pets.

It is very important in spirit communication that you have an open mind and a hopeful attitude. Interaction will and can happen because if one begins with predisposed beliefs the dead do not talk, do not exist after physical death, then one is not keeping an open mind. Become the observer. Be open to whatever occurs. Remember the information you receive, observe, hear, imagine or think about can be examined later. Then you can assess the information and decide if it is meaningful to you and if it helps your peace of mind and spiritual awareness.

What is to be Considered to Conduct a Séance: Three important factors must be considered when conducting a séance: the purpose, the quality of the sitters and the location. Each of these must be prepared to increase the possibilities of a reasonably successful outcome and pleasant union with spirit. Helpful and basic conditions are listed below.

• The Purpose: Establish this prior to the séance. Whatever the purpose, the participants must focus on it only. Especially for a smaller, more private affair, divided purposes in the circle can weaken or destroy singleness of psychic energy needed in the séance. The conducting medium will query each sitter and make him or her understand the importance of a single mind. This is not always possible with a larger group.

• Attitude of the Participants or Sitters: Desire to be there is the primary qualification for a sitter. If someone has to be dragged into the circle, it's wrong. The greater number of sincere participants in the group, the better the results will be.

Those who want to be there, who are serious and not frivolous or silly and giddy should be in the circle. Positive and uplifting people add energy like those who are empathetic and can inject love into the séance. Love is the key to communication in the spirit world. Its presence enables communication to take place. The level of openness in a group is important for a successful outcome and will heighten the connection between medium and spirit. For this reason, test séances are seldom successful. Even if the people are there in good faith but have prejudiced thoughts, negative results may occur unless the medium is exceptional with excellent spiritual relationships and support from the spirit world. Thoughts and efforts need to be in accord for easier communication. Even one person with contradictory or antagonistic thoughts can retard the sincere efforts of the sensitive. One time, a colleague planned a spirit communication for a group of twenty-five people with me as the medium. In time, I got annoyed dealing with the stops and starts and negative vibrations in the room. I asked who was it that thought this was a bunch of bunk? A man confessed his wife dragged him and he didn't believe in any of it. I invited him to leave. He did and we successfully continued.

The skeptical and cynical person can drain the entire circle of its energy and the result fulfills the skeptic's expectations. Even if it is a family member, do not allow this person to be a part of it. A fear-filled person has almost the same effect as the skeptic. Fear is a great negative, which has a counter effect to the positive love vibration. Their fear may be self-generated or the results of religious superstition, nevertheless, avoid this person. Anyone full of hate or envy against anyone in the circle or outside of it will have a deleterious effect on a séance.

A family member who wants to contact a deceased loved one must not be grasping and groping for the connection. Rather, they should be subjective and patient for whatever comes. Desperate people can block the energy; they must put their feelings in check and be neutral. This is why I suggest not participating in spirit communication until one has some control over one's grief. Avoid dwelling on any one thought, especially sorrowful ones. Be careful to not become overly eager, anxious or stressed. Be natural and relaxed mentally and physically.

In a larger group that takes place in an auditorium or large church with a celebrity medium like John Edwards or The Long Island Medium, the audience has paid a decent price to participate and therefore I'm sure there aren't too many hardcore skeptics in attendance.

Open your mind, feel peace, joy and love to help the energy change to a higher vibration. Before you begin to communicate take time to relax. Alone, or with the group, you can sing or chant at intervals as it creates a friendlier atmosphere and a more cheerful frame of mind. It also attracts the spiritual forces. If you are not in the correct state of mind, are emotionally upset, mentally tired, scattered, in a state of confusion, and/or physically weak, your spirit communication will be compromised and most likely will not produce desired positive results. Your mental and physical highs and lows influence your spirit communication as well as the kinds of spirits you attract. You want the proper energy before attempting to communicate with spirit. Begin by preparing yourself through proper nutritious food, rest, and meditation to quiet the mind, balance the emotions and release stress from the body. Stop if you feel troubled or fearful of the spirit communication. You are either not ready or have contacted a spirit that you are not prepared to handle. If for any reason you find you have contacted undesirable spirits, it is highly recommended you have a true forceful medium take care of the situation. To help avoid this situation, say aloud at the beginning of your séance you invite only loving and kind spirits to visit.

• Séance Set-up: Séance or spirit communication is more successful when two or more people gather for the purpose of connecting in hopes of receiving information or a message. There is strength in union. It can be a private séance with family and/or close friends or a larger public event held in a spiritualist church, hall, or other meeting place. Seating can be with fold-up chairs, pews, couches, on the floor, or around a table, holding hands, or fingertips touching. When two people are together, sit opposite each other––for three people, form a triangle and four or more, a circle. If you are in a larger group, the medium will most likely sit on a platform and the group will either encircle or face the medium.

Although it is usual during a séance for one person to act as the medium, sometimes all participants may wish to mediate messages. If you wish to mediate a séance, it would be wise to do so only under the direction of a trained medium for the first few times. The medium should be one who has already presided over a séance and is familiar with the importance of insuring the basic requirements are met. She will attract the energies as well as lend you strength and clarity during the communication. A non-experienced person may conduct the séance however the outcome may be affected because of a lack of attunement. A developed medium is not essential to your success if you feel the power lies dormant within you and you are sincere. In either case, it is up to the conducting medium to assure the conditions outlined are met.

• Location: There are two best choices. The first is in a neutral location free from outside disturbances, noises, and interference, preferably one previously used for such a purpose. Next is a place with a symbolic connection to the purpose. For example, the home of a deceased person you're trying to establish contact with, because it will have objects and artifacts, which still have their owner's imprint on them. Incidentally, personal artifacts can also be brought to a neutral meeting place.

• Gathering for the séance: Wait until everyone is present. Then sit around and make small talk for about twenty minutes. This gives everyone time to settle down and get accustomed to the setting. Then you can begin.

• The séance format: For a smaller group, everyone should sit in a circle, either around a table or with straight back chairs. They should be close enough to hold hands. The lights should be dim or candles lit. There should be enough light to see everyone's face. It is not necessary to conduct the meeting in total darkness. After a period of relaxation most participants might close their eyes. This is perfectly fine and adds to a calmer physical and mental condition. For a larger, or more casual meeting, people can sit on couches, on comfortable seating, or on the floor.

For at least ten minutes, soft meditative music playing in the background or singing together lightens the mood and raises the vibration of the participants. The conducting medium reminds all present the love vibration carries communication and to invoke it now. The purpose of the séance is spoken aloud.

In the case of seeking spirit guides, everyone is reminded to remember any feelings, visions and thoughts they receive in the session to share with all present. For the purpose of conjuring apparitions, the same instructions are given. When the séance is to invoke a deceased person's spirit, the same rules apply, except they are told to send the love vibration to the spirit sought and hold the person in loving remembrance.

Participants should be cautioned about any silly or frivolous message or information. If it cannot be confirmed it is the personality of a spirit known to a participant that spirit should be firmly rejected. It can be a troublesome, such as a poltergeist, (troublesome spirit) coming to disturb the sincerity of the séance. Wait for something more substantial.

For 20 to 30 minutes, everyone should stay in this loving remembrance state. Then they are softly requested to return their attention to the circle and open their eyes when ready.

After a few minutes they should all be alert and ready to talk. The medium starts anywhere in the circle and encourages everyone to share their experience. What the medium looks for is profound information with evidence of a connection. Duplicate messages, visions or feelings, are confirmations of a connection with the spirit.

A recording can be made during the message part for future reference. Don't expect a voice to emanate from the corner of the room or from within an object. This only happens in the movies. Remember those in spirit must try just as hard as we do in order to communicate. It's not easy for the dead or the living to communicate. For the spirits to be heard or understood, imagine a bad telephone connection with static, or speaking to another in a foreign language trying to get their point across. In the latter situation it's not words, it's in gestures and/or images. When you have communicated a few times, you will understand what is needed. Séances sometimes require repeat sessions for sufficient details to piece together a coherent picture. Be patient.

For conjuring a particular spirit, whether once a living person or a spiritual being such as a teacher or angel, a medium will look for the number of similarities in the sitters' information or desires. This strengthens the success of reaching the spirit. Many times, there are a number of people who receive the same message, vision or feeling during the session. These are confirmations of a single spirit's influence during the séance.

To help you create a positive and successful spirit communication, I highly recommend you first establish and practice a strong and continuous communication with your own spiritual self. Doing so helps you know your strengths, weaknesses, fears and superstitions about the spirit world. Daily meditation and reading a spiritual quote or adage will keep you centered and give purpose to your life.

Do not become dependent upon séances or a medium for spirit communication nor have séances too often. Sitting for a séance should not be more than once a month. Learn to listen with the inner ear for a hello or a peaceful message in dreams and at other quiet times. You can also feel the presence of spirit as a hug or stroke of a hand if you sit still open up and invite a dead loved one to give you an embrace.

Limit the séance to one hour lest they drain your nervous system. Start with a noise free darkened candle lit room. This allows you to learn how to quiet yourself and not be distracted by external influences. Some think séances should only be held at nighttime believing light stops spiritual forces. Although it is true it is stiller at night and people relax more in a darker, candlelight atmosphere, it is not necessary for successful communication. Darkness can be beneficial for developing mediums (or sensitives) to help calm and center their thoughts. In time, you will know the best and most comfortable way for you. The room for séances should be absolutely free from any disturbing noises, such as a clock ticking, phones ringing, people coming and going or creaking rocking chairs. Members should sit upright, be comfortable and place both feet on the floor. The crossing of the feet or slouching in a chair interferes with the bodily currents and tends to break and slow the forces. The sitters need not hold hands. If the sitters wish to, the right hand is placed palm up and the left hand covers the next sitter's right hand, which is palm up. Holding hands generates a flow of energy between sitters and they, in essence, become one vibration. Sitters can touch fingertips if they do not wish to hold hands.

It can be tiring after a period of time. Unless the participants are accustomed to sitting still for long periods of time, they will become uncomfortable and begin to fidget. Again, the length of the séance might be too long for a comfortable sitting. For successful results, occupy the same place on each occasion. If after several attempts, manifestations do not appear or telepathic messages are not given, change positions. The new positioning may create the proper vibrational energy between certain sitters needed for contact.

You may want to add a photograph of the person you wish to contact. Ask the medium where to place it.

Though, not as popular as they once were, billets can be used during a séance. I had forgotten about this form of connecting with spirit until Sheila Medina, who was a childhood friend of mine, and I reunited many years later at the Golden Gate Spiritual Church in San Francisco. To my surprise she too had been gifted with the ability to communicate with spirits. She invited me to a séance she was conducting with the use of billets. A billet is a written name and a question for the spirit the participant wishes to contact. The paper is folded, the participant's name written on the outside, and it's placed in a box for the medium to select. She reads the name on the outside and shares the message from the spirit. The question might not be answered nor the spirit the participant asked for to come through, but no doubt communication will occur.

Some spiritualist organizations have more than one medium hosting a séance. There can be two or more mediums delivering messages. Most participants receive a message. I suggest you remain open and accept the message. There's time after to figure it out. If after a while the message continues to have no meaning to you, let it be considered as misdirected or misunderstood communication.

To aid your preparations for the right conditions, remember to say an invocation, chant, or sing a song as an opening to your ritual. Here is one from *The Grandmother of Time* by Z. (Zsuzsanna) Budapest, I like to recite:

> *I am the channel of divine insight in the universe.*
> *My inner eyes see what my god sees.*
> *My inner ears hear what my god hears.*
> *My inner heart loves what my god loves.*

■ ■ ■

8

SOLO

The dead live. How do they live? By love.

— John Fowles, Magus —

We have discussed group communication, but you can certainly have equally, if not more so, rewarding and spiritually enlightening experiences by yourself. Stay open to messages from your loved ones coming, not only in words, but in dreams, symbols, memories, and chance encounters. If for any reason you find you contacted undesirable spirits, it is highly recommended that a trained and forceful medium take care of the situation.

Stay open to receiving messages from spirits you hadn't planned on talking with. People have come to me with one particular person in mind. They did all the homework, brought photos, and wrote simple questions. Their intended spirit didn't come through but another did, such as a grammar school teacher.

In preparation for spirit communication it is most important you learn to be quiet and listen. Most of us are good at talking and not so good at listening. This holds true with communicating with a spirit. Think about a conversation where one person talks endlessly, throws in a question or two but never takes a breath to let you answer. This is how it usually sounds to the dead, spirits, angels, God, Allah, Buddha, or whomever, when people talk to them. All that chatting, pleading, ranting, crying, directing! Once you have spoken, be still, listen, be aware, be patient.

For positive and successful spirit communication I highly recommend you first establish and practice a strong and continuous communication with your own self, your spirit. Take time to know your strengths and weaknesses physically, emotionally, mentally, and spiritually. Then you can recognize your energy when it is in a high or low level. This does influence your spirit communication and the kinds of spirit energy you attract. Daily meditation is a wonderful way to calm your mind, body and emotions to connect with your spirit.

Meditation is an altered state of consciousness. In it, the body is completely relaxed, the emotions calm and the mind free of busy, everywhere thoughts. With no schedule to keep, our minds drift from troubles and daily responsibilities. Meditation is an excellent way to enter the pathway of spirit communication. In fact before beginning my spirit sessions or ghost encounters, I always prepare with meditation. Keep it simple. Learning to meditate is easy, doing it can be a true challenge. It requires you to stop moving and free your mind of constant thoughts. I suggest you start out slowly with five to ten minutes of relaxing the body through some easy stretching and deep breathing. Then sit comfortably on the floor, or in a straight back chair (if you lay down you might fall asleep and this is not mediation) for another five or ten minutes. Again, take a few deep easy breaths. The challenge is the many thoughts that flow through the mind. To help you release those thoughts focus on a single object like a candle flame, a flower, a simple photograph or an art piece. The relief of stress through meditation does wonders for your health physically and mentally, however it is also while in a meditative state, many insights happen even if at the time you don't realize they have. It's one of the powers and advantages of meditation.

There are several ways to communicate with spirit energy whether it is the spirit of a deceased loved one, spirit guides or other spirit entities. Most people wish to communicate with their departed loved ones while a few want to hear from the historically famous. This happened once in the many séances I have been involved with over the years.

At first, I was uncertain if I should mention seeing Ronald Reagan in spirit. There was no reason for me to think of him. I don't recall his movies, nor did I vote for him; but in my mental image he appeared as a young, smiling man. He said nothing. I ventured forth and shared whom I saw. One participant laughed and said, "He was a friend of my grandfather when they were young." Then I laughed, relieved. She had a story of her grandfather and Ronald Reagan. This was my first and last historical figure experience.

Spirit interaction occurs anywhere, at any time and for me, even in a supermarket aisle. Although in most circumstances it is best to set a time, place and situation for spirit communication.

I believe the absolutely best and most comforting way to speak and share time with your beloved dead is on your own. Sadly, during times of grief your emotional pain usually makes communicating most difficult. Often times you cry, huddle under the covers, so fragile emotionally you close yourself off from the outside world. In a shocked, depressed state, you seek solace from mediums to connect you with your dead.

A medium can certainly be most helpful when you are in this state. In time you can contact your loved one on your own. The challenge is to calm your emotions and sit quietly to allow the flow of energies, between you, the living, and the spirit of your deceased. Do not doubt you will feel contact. Be comforted, accepting. Perhaps share your experience with another person connected to the spirit. The same, or a similar message may have come to them.

Before communicating, take some time to relax. Sing or chant to create a friendlier atmosphere and a happier more cheerful frame of mind. It also is attractive to the spiritual forces. If you feel too troubled––stop!

When you are past the first stages of grief, go to a serene setting. This can be a room or garden in your home, or a place in nature, perhaps a place you shared with your loved one. Settle in and settle down. Feel energy shift around you. Be aware of the room temperature. Temperatures change when the spirit moves into the space. Quietly say the name of the spirit you wish to contact aloud three times. In your relaxed state wait for your loved one to visit and remain open to whatever you sense and/or mentally hear, see or feel. It could be a thought, a word(s). You may see the spirit in the movement of nature or mentally see your loved one's face. You may know, without a doubt, your loved one is with you in that moment. Unless you have a clear understanding of the message try not to decipher it. It might be a symbol, a sign, an image, a memory you shared or a person you don't recognize. There will be time to sort it out or it will become clear to you at a later date. Accept if you do not experience a spirit visit or message. Perhaps at another time you will.

• Special Room——Psychomanteum: In Dr. Raymond Moody's book, *Reunions* (1994) he writes about a room or a chamber he invented and named *psychomanteum* (mirror gazing) for the purpose of communicating with spirits of the dead. The chamber was inspired by the technique for spirit encounters used 2500 years ago at the Oracle of the Dead in Ephyra, Greece. The Greeks sat in darkened caves with a candle and a mirror or a bowl of water to gaze into in hopes of seeing an image of their dead materialize. It became known as mirror gazing. In an on-line article, Necromanteion: Oracle of the Dead in Greece: Sailing up the mysterious Acheron River to the Greek Underworld of Hades by Rob MacGregor, he writes, "Very little was known about the Greek psychomanteums until 1958 when archaeologist Sotirios Dakaris and his team uncovered a series of small underground rooms connected by a passageway that led to the main chamber where they found the remains of a large copper cauldron ringed with a banister.

They had discovered the Oracle of the Dead, spoken of by Homer and Herodotus."

Dr. Moody, in his research of those who had NDE and visitations from spirits viewed the room as a therapeutic tool to heal grief and bring insight. It was set up to optimize psychological effects such as entering into a trance. The room was free of any external sounds and completely dark, or with only a flickering candle. Flickering candles or lamps are sometimes recommended to induce hallucination. The dimness represents a form of visual sensory deprivation, a condition helpful to trance induction. In the room is a chair for the communicator and a mirror, or as in ancient times, a still pool of water, for spirit energy to reveal its presence. Reflective objects, such as a mirror, and surfaces, as still water, were considered in ancient times to be a conduit to the spirit world. The person gazes into the mirror or water hoping an apparition or vision materializes.

When you enter the room, light the candle if there is one. Relax and greet whomever you wish to contact, then gaze into the mirror or water. Stay in the room for about fifteen minutes, but no more than one hour because it's too demanding on the mind and body. Personally, I have had many substantial spirit communications in well-lit places. Only over time will you know what is most comfortable for you.

• Mirror Gazing: If you wish to experiment with mirror gazing you don't need a psychomanteum, although your experience can be more fulfilling if you choose a space where you won't be interrupted. Turn off telephone ringers. Leave pets outside the room because they may want attention and disturb your meditative state. Have a mirror large enough to view your face easily. If it's dark in the room, have a candle or a soft light. You can sit or stand but the mirror must be at eye level so you don't look down or gaze up at it. Quiet your thoughts. Close your eyes and think of a peaceful place in nature. After a while, turn your mind to the person you want to communicate with. In your mind imagine or see the person you wish to make contact with. You might think of a photograph or a time when you were looking at her or him. Make the image as clear as possible until you can see their features. Smile at the person then slowly open your eyes halfway and gaze into the mirror. Imagine the image in your mind appears in the mirror. Do your best to keep your mind focused, but if it should drift and the mirror image is not complete or blurry, that's okay. Relax, breathe. Feel your mind and heart open up to communicating with the spirit. If you have a question, ask it aloud or in your mind. Wait for your answer. It can come as a word, or a feeling and even as an image or symbol.

• Dreams: The easiest and gentlest way of contacting those who have passed is through dreams. Many people who have a dream or recurring dreams, about dead relatives and friends ask if I think they are indeed communicating. I say yes. The brain is still a scientific mystery. No one knows how powerful and abstract it is and what can be perceived. Can it be in sleep we are free to see and hear on different levels than in an awakened state? I believe the answer is yes. In an altered state of consciousness we are without all the barriers of doubts and beliefs and open to spirit interaction. Pay particular attention to any words, gestures or symbols in the dreams. The spirit may be reminding you of a particular time you shared, comforting you, or just showing up to say, "hello."

• Nature is a perfect healing source, a wonderful place to be with your own spirit and of those surrounding you. Go to a favorite quiet spot in nature where you can relax and let go of the outside world. Nature provides simply beautiful messages from beyond in symbolic ways like a bird or butterfly landing on your shoulder. I was with a friend at the California Academy of Sciences Rainforest. It is full of screeching scarlet macaws, cute hummingbirds, and beautiful multi-colored butterflies. The balmy temperature was like the Brazilian rainforest I visited a few years earlier. Despite the beauty surrounding me, my heart was heavy with sadness. I spoke silently to my sister who departed for her heavenly home a few months earlier, "I wish I could know you made it to the other side. I wish you'd give me a sign." Within a second two huge butterflies landed on my hair. The butterflies intertwined, fluttering their wings. I laughed and thought of her playful ways and how intertwined our lives had been. My companion took it as proof! Nature provides comfort, heals and connects you to spirit. Close your eyes. Open your ears. Listen to the rustle of the tree's leaves. Feel the roll of the ocean waves. Eavesdrop on the birds' chatter. In this state of quietness, you will know and feel the presence of spirit. You might feel a hand on your hand, the warmth of a hug. Be in the moment. Simple, small movements, signs and gentle energy are how most spirits let you know they are with you.

We are a part of nature, and to the earth, the sky and the ocean we return. "*From my rotting body, flowers shall grow and I am in them and this is eternity.*" – Edvard Munch.

• Automatic Writing: Though I have experimented with automatic writing it was difficult to read the results. You may have better luck. Automatic writing or psychography is a psychic ability, which produces written words without consciously writing. The words are said to come from the subconscious, spiritual essence or supernatural source. Automatic writing happens in a trance or waking state. While in a relaxed state the writer passively holds a pencil on a sheet of paper to allow messages to flow from the subconscious mind. Spiritualists believe the spirits take control of the hand to write messages, letters and even entire books like *Letters From the Other Side: With Love, Harry and Helen* by Mary Blunt White. I not only enjoyed reading this book very much, but found it quite enlightening. Arthur Conan Doyle in his book *The New Revelation* (1918) wrote, "...automatic writing occurs either by the writer's subconscious or by external spirits operating through the writer." Thomas Jay Hudson, a psychical researcher, said no spirits are involved in automatic writing and it is the subconscious mind, which produces the information or messages. Since you have become more aware of how the subconscious mind drives your life decisions, there may be other powers and abilities it possesses. If you want to decide if automatic writing is a way for you to connect with the dead, experiment with it in your psychomanteum.

• A Helper: Spirits do send messages and help through another. This can be a family member, a friend or even someone you don't know or know well at all. As hard as we try, sometimes the spirit just can't get through to us. Not only at a group session——a séance——might another person receive a message for you, but in other ways such as what happened with my mother. She had heart surgery and her recovery wasn't going well. She wasn't responding as the doctors had hoped. Along with some of my family members, I asked for help from the other side. No messages were received. No doubt we were all too emotional. On the night before Thanksgiving, I went to the Golden Gate Spiritualist Church in San Francisco. There were three mediums; one was Scottish like my family. Before she took the podium, I saw the spirits of my maternal grandparents sitting in an aisle across from me. When the Scottish medium spoke, she went directly to me saying the whole clan was with me. By first name she called out the names of my mother's parents, aunts and brothers. It was a long list! Tears rolled down my cheeks. I couldn't even speak although it is requested when a medium focuses on you to say hello or thank you. The medium said my mother hadn't decided to stay or leave, but help was coming.

The following day when I visited my mother, which was Thanksgiving. I learned that I had a wonderful reason to be thankful! I was surprised to see her sitting up with color back in her face. She told me a Scottish male nurse came in the night before and told her to stop lying around and get up. My mother said that just hearing the Scottish voice rallied her. She went on to say he wasn't scheduled to be on duty, but the night nurse called in sick. After my mother came home, we called the number the male nurse had left. The person said there was no one with that name there. We never did check with the hospital but believe an angel in the form of a human was sent to keep my mother alive. Whether he was an angel or spirit, or human, he did as the medium said, helped my mother.

• Symbols and Signs: Humans can be so dense, unaware, and unable to believe in any message from the spirits which isn't verbal communication. Phooey, they say if communication or a sighting isn't exactly how they image it should be, when over and over they've given you a sign. In the past and still now, certain cultures like Native Americans believe nature provides signs and messages about upcoming events as well as spirits. As I said above, nature connects to our true spirit and to the spirits of the departed in a refreshing calm way. There are other signs. Once a woman in a store answered a question I had just asked a dead fashion diva friend. The woman pointed to one of the two blouses I was holding up, unsure of which to choose. She picked the color and style my friend would have. A bit loud and low cut for my usual taste. I bought it, people loved it on me and I thanked my friend. What signs and symbols have you thought came from spirits?

■ ■ ■

9

MEDIUMS

There is a land of the living and a land of the dead and the bridge is love, the only survival, the only meaning.

— Thornton Wilder —

For the sake of ease, I'll use the term medium rather than psychic and/or psychic reader. Not all psychic readers are mediums. A medium specifically talks to the spirit of the dead and/or picks up the energy of other non-living entities. Some psychic readers can mediate between the spirit of the dead and the living although their focus is on giving clients information about the past (including past lives) and certainly about future events. When consulting with a medium do not expect you will be given information about future outcomes to a problem or issue you might have. The medium can present advice from the other side to help you along with an issue, but certainly will not make a prediction like a psychic reader. I will also refer to the medium as she, although there are very talented male mediums such as John Edwards and James Van Praagh.

One successful way for spirits to communicate is through a medium, or also can be known as a channel, sensitive, or clairvoyant. This person uses her *clairsenses* (clair is derived from the French word for clear thus clear senses and corresponds with the five physical senses). She uses her clairsenses to communicate with nonphysical energy through sensing or feeling, seeing, hearing, tasting and smelling without using physical sensors. The medium relays information about a person, animal, place, or object without prior knowledge. This energy or information, history, can be someone or something close to the person inquiring, or of a place or time long passed or at a great distance. She is the go-between of the two worlds—the living, you and the spirit, the dead or the unseen. The medium accepts the presence of the spirits who have passed on from the physical plane to another plane of existence, often referred to as Heaven, Nirvana, or The Other World. The medium may offer you a private session or invite you to participate in a group. The group may vary in size.

There are different levels of mediumship and various ways she receives information. She can be a clairvoyant, which means clear sight—*voyant*—light, to make vision possible. She can clearly see a person, place, thing or event without the physical use of eyes. This is also known as "second sight." She might mentally see past, future, or present events, in her mind's eye as an image, a picture, symbol, as though watching a film or reading words like in a book and/or colors. She may also receive a vision or a prophetic dream about a situation, event or person.

A clairvoyant medium can help educate a person with clairvoyant abilities who have imaged negative, fearful entities and events. People have often asked me about visions or dreams that have had that disturbed them; ones where something bad was going to happen. It is rare people who have these kind of images or dreams listen to or act on their visions and more so than not, the worst doesn't happen how it was dreamt or envisioned. If what they envisioned became a tragedy, like an accident or grave illness they often say, "I should have done something to stop it." In actuality, it is rare a tragedy or accident can be halted because people usually will not take such warnings seriously. A trained medium is wise in her presentation of delivering not so pleasant insights. She can prepare a person for the potentially challenging situation, but also would want to give a positive way of handling it.

With one client I saw his wife, who had cancer, would die in a couple of months. They knew her death was imminent. I told him to prepare and complete all necessary paperwork such as a will, insurance information, and burial decisions and arrangement within thirty days so they could enjoy time together without worrying about those kinds of responsibilities. He did and they had the next month to focus on enjoying their time left together. After the funeral he contacted me to ask if I saw her death so soon after taking care of all the business and if so, why didn't I tell him when it would happen? I answered with, "If I told you, would you have been relieved or anxious, dreading her end the whole time?"

He understood that my advice to prepare paper work and enjoy his time with her was best for both of them. Some upcoming events will not be prevented and therefore knowing when and how doesn't add to life, rather it can take away one's peace of mind.

The medium may be a *clairaudient,* which means, "clear listener or clear sound"—*audient,* one who pays attention, who listens. The medium hears sounds, which exist beyond the reach of the physical ears (inaudible to the physical ear), as the voices of the dead. She hears information psychically as if conversing with someone or listening into a conversation. The ability is called *clairaudio*; clear hearing. If this message is not for her, she passes it to whoever is participating in the communication session. A medium can deliver messages in the spirit's voice if she is willing to channel directly, which is not as easy or comfortable as one would think. Her voice will be unlike her own often and often different in speech patterns, tones, or wording. The words might be an older version of speech, very proper or words not used in modern day English. The tone changes also and even her mannerisms such as facial or body gestures differ than her own. If the clairaudient chooses not to use direct voice known as *channeling the spirit in voice* she will interpret what she heard in her own voice, and most likely in her/his own words. Therefore, the message may not be in the tone, inflection or language of the dead person but is no less accurate or important. It's a choice a medium makes based on her preference and perhaps level of skill to use direct voice, or channel, means sharing the body—vocal cords—with the spirit. It can open up the possibility of the spirit or entity not vacating the medium's space (physical body) at the end of the message. When this happens, it takes a toll on a medium's mental, emotional, and physical state. Therefore, mediums do their best work when trained and educated in self-protection, and clearing energy after each spirit communication or psychic reading session. I have allowed very few spirits to channel through me. Instead, I chose to stay in control of my own spirit and body.

The clairaudient can become unnerved with hearing voices no one else does. They think it can't be tuned out. It can, or at least can be managed. Chanting and meditation will be a great help to manage this ability. The majority of mediums I know or know of, meditate and pray before sessions.

Mediums, as you can imagine, are very sensitive to all seen and unseen, known and unknown, thus the term sensitives, or *clairsentients* and also can be referred to as a *clairempathy*. This ability is known as *clairsentience*—sentience from the Latin word sentine, to feel. They are keenly perceptive with strong, acute emotional responses to whomever and whatever they come in contact with. The German philosopher Rudolf Lotze coined the word, which comes from empathy, in 1858. He believed when you look at a work of art, you project your own sensibilities onto it. When a clairsentient has an intuitive feeling about a person, living or dead, spirit, or an occurrence, past, present or future, there is a physical reaction. She may experience hair rising on the back of her neck or on her arms alerting her of a psychic impression. She may experience a tightening in the gut or a headache developing and may say, "*I just had a feeling*" or, "*I had a hunch*" or, "*My gut told me*" or, "*Someone walked over my grave.*"

Empathetic mediums often will hold hands or touch the client to connect to the information.

In my many years as a psychic/medium consultant and teacher of ESP/psychic development, I have found clairsentience is the most difficult of the ESP abilities to manage. It's been my experience that most clairsentients have difficulty articulating their feelings and thoughts. The psychic energy is like a strong electrical jolt, which leaves the recipient stunned, and tingling. The feeling usually does not provide the clairsentient an image or picture or a mental word message. In classes, I taught clairsentients to give their intuitive feelings a color, then an image and finally a description to decipher what they picked-up through the use of the mind or intellect. This is not to say only clairsentience have difficulty with psychic impressions. A trained medium understands how to observe the message rather than take the feelings into her body as her own. Untrained, and at times even trained and professional clairempathics (clear feelers) can unfortunately suffer another's maladies. She experiences the same mental, emotional and physical conditions of another. In the beginning of my awakening to my psychic abilities I experienced this at times. My client would leave free of her/his ills, but only I retained them until I learned how not to. For more on empathics see my ESP quiz.

Some mediums might also experience *clairgustance*––gustance the essence of a substance as in a sensation of smelling or tasting which does not physically exist in the immediate surroundings. For example she might psychically smell a toxic odor and the inquiring person knows the spirit in question died from a dangerous chemical overdose. Or, the medium might pick up the scent of a dog and go on to describe it. The inquiring person had wanted to know about her pet in spirit.

Most mediums can communicate with your pet's spirit just as easily as with a human spirit. If that is of interest to you, ask before your schedule an appointment if she does that. At your appointment you can choose a few questions with answers you already know to see if the medium has made the connection. For instance you might ask if your pet continues to enjoy her or his favorite sleeping area, or does Fido or Kit Kat miss his or her favorite toy?

A medium, no matter how the impressions are experienced, once aware of her psychic abilities, can learn to stop or expel energy so as not to be a helpless victim of it.

I have heard from quite a few people who are having visitations from spirits and at times, vampire entities. They feel no power to stop these visitations. Most spirit/ghost hauntings are quite harmless. Start out by asking the spirit to quiet down (if its noisy) or stop moving things (if objects are moved or disappear). Wait a day or so and see if that helped. If not, here are some ways to stop or ease up the intensity of them: Smudge (with a smudge stick or use incense, e.g. Frankincense, rose, or sandalwood) to clean your energy and the space/room where the visitations take place. With the smudge stick (or incense) starting from your feet up to your head and back down wave it back and forth. Some smudge sticks are overly smoky, and might not be good for you. Doing this is somewhat like taking a shower. Then, do the same to the space where the visitations take place. Once you've completed that, and if you feel or see the spirit, look at it and be direct by saying aloud, it's time for you to leave this space or remove yourself from my space. You might have to do this a few times. If the energy or visitations intensify and you become fearful of it, call in a medium accustom to removing spirits. If it's indeed a low-grade or vampire entity, be sure to have a medium that can deal with that kind of energy.

This is why education and training for those with strong ESP abilities is so very important. With a greater understanding for why they feel or experience what they do, how to communicate it successfully and how it can be a wonderful source of comfort and healing for others, psychic mediums can enjoy their abilities and talents.

A medium can easily sense and communicate nonphysical spirits for insight about herself. The added benefit is the joy of sharing these insights with family, friends and, perhaps, even strangers to answer their questions. The ESP quiz in Chapter 12 will help you determine your personal abilities and how to advance them.

■ ■ ■

10

THE VEIL DROPS: HALLOWEEN AND DAY OF THE DEAD RITUAL

Hark! Hark to the wind! 'Tis the night, they say,
When all souls come back from the far away
The dead, forgotten this many a day!

— Virna Sheard, Poet —

Halloween, a spooky good time and all for amusement, right? The night is much more than just for fun. All Hallows Eve or Halloween and November First, are sacred times for many throughout the world to honor the dead. The Celts and Mexicans honor their elderly, ancestors, and the dead with special rituals and celebrations on those days. The Catholic Church combined the pagan beliefs with their own to create a day to honor the saints on November first. Celtic pagans believed the veils between the two worlds of the living and dead thinned or dropped so spirits could walk the earth to visit their living relatives before crossing back over to the *underworld*.

The spirits were not only our loved ones, but also all spirits who want to walk the earth, feel alive and connected to the living. During the spirits' visit, spooky things happened, as you can imagine. The Celts disguised themselves to waylay troublesome or evil spirits so they wouldn't recognize and haunt people. Tradition warned people, especially the elderly, the sick and the young, to stay safely hidden inside so they wouldn't be grabbed and taken to the underworld or netherworld (an otherworld deep underground or beneath the surface of the world where souls of the departed go after life.)

This is a good time to invite the spirits you want to visit. You can prepare with one of these welcoming rituals; one more elaborate and the other, simple. You can do all or a bit of each. Design a ritual to best suit your interest and need. No matter which you choose to do, both are a lovely way to remember your loved ones and feel their presence.

Before it is dark on Halloween get a photograph of the deceased you would like to visit and a pen in perhaps their favorite color. You'll also need paper, flowers and incense of your choice. Also gather white, black and orange candles. The white candle is for protection and to receive clear visions. The black candle is for the mystical, spiritual unknown, and the orange one for the season's color of renewal. Have a burning vessel (ashtray or cauldron,) matches to light your incense and candles, and a full lipped glass or bowl of water. The water signifies the other world and also can be used to douse any fire mishaps. In a nice glass or cup pour a beverage, (perhaps one the spirits you wish to visit liked when alive). Include a sweet treat. The drink and treat are symbolic of hospitality for your visiting spirit guests. Optional item is a cloth to lay the items on. Have two chairs available, one for you and one for the spirit to sit (hopefully only one spirit shows at a time) and visit. Set-up your items near a window. Or, you can simply light a white candle, and place it in a window along with a beverage and treat. Your spirits seeing the candlelight will recognize your home.

Peer into the water, relax and connect to the psychic mind. Perhaps an image will form or a memory will be recalled. Afterwards, invite your spirits to visit. Stay as long as you like, thinking of your loved ones, talking to them. If you hear, think or sense a message given, take note of it for later examination. Or you may dream about the spirits after your ritual (remember to snuff the candles and incense). It's easier for them to communicate in this way. Once you lay out your items, light your incense and candles. Quiet yourself for a few minutes or longer and then say aloud, "Only good can enter herein." Perhaps add a prayer to the Divine to bring forth healing, loving energies and protect you from negative fearful thoughts and/or energies. After all, it is Halloween and negative energies/entities also roam free along with your loved ones' spirits. To the best of your ability, endeavor to be calm and peaceful.

When you feel relaxed, take up your pen and paper and list all those who have passed, and how they affected your life. I write a thank you to my departed loved ones for what they shared and fostered in my life, love, support, talents, and knowledge. To my ancestors, I acknowledge the blessings such as the abilities and skills passed down to help me to live fully. You can fold the paper and put it by the photographs. You can burn your message in your fire safe bowl. As the paper burns, it turns into rising smoke, symbolic for sending your thoughts to the mental psychic airwaves. It's like 'mailing your message.' Or, fold and keep it overnight to burn later or bury or throw in a moving body of water. The ashes are also buried or thrown in to water.

I keep my candles lit until bedtime before I snuff them out or extinguish them if I'm leaving the house. If perhaps you haven't felt the presence of your loved one and would like to keep your candles burning all night you can place them in your bathtub. Make sure there is nothing flammable, like a towel or washcloth within reach of the flames. You may get a message for another. If you do, share it. Spirit communication is often stronger with more than one person. Perhaps someone may want to join you.

Wishing you a frolicking good time and a cauldron full of happy spirit communication!

■ ■ ■

11

GHOST HUNTS

There is something haunting in the light of the moon.

– Joseph Conrad –

Throughout history, ghost encounters and haunted houses have thrilled many people. Wide-eyed children and breath-holding adults sit around darkened rooms listening to spooky stories, hanging on every ghoulish detail and shrieking at the Big Moment of Fright. People line up at amusement parks to ride into dark tunnels where the *unknown* awaits to thrill them. Movies with girls screaming, and boys hiding their screams behind nervous giggles have been popular since the first three minute horror movie, "Le Manoir du Diable", by George Melies, in 1896.

To this day, when I shower in a motel, I peek out to make sure no knife wielding man is coming to stab me as in Alfred

Hitchcock's "Psycho." Yet, fear doesn't keep me from visiting graveyards or old haunted buildings, and I've been to plenty. If you're like me, you visit these places too, whether on your own, with friends, or on a tour.

Since ancient times, tales of hauntings figure prominently in the folklore of almost every culture throughout the world. These sightings include historical figures, queens, politicians, writers and gangsters, many of who died early, violent or mysterious deaths.

One of the most frequently reported ghost sightings is Anne Boleyn, wife of England's King Henry VIII and mother of Queen Elizabeth I. She was executed at the Tower of London in May 1536 after accusations of witchcraft, treason, incest and adultery. Reportedly, her ghost is seen in the Tower and drifting through her childhood home, Hever Castle, in Kent, England.

An earlier report of ghosts in the house was made in the first century A.D. by the great Roman author and statesman, Pliny the Younger. He recorded one of the first notable ghost stories in his letters. He reported the specter [ghost] of an old man with a long beard, rattling chains, haunted his house in Athens. The Greek writer Lucian also wrote memorable ghost stories.

In Germany, 856 A.D. the first poltergeist, a ghost who causes physical disturbances such as loud noises or objects falling or being thrown around, was reported at a farmhouse. The poltergeist tormented the family living there by throwing stones and starting fires, among other things.

Beginning in the late 19th century, Benjamin Franklin's ghost has been seen near the library of the American

Philosophical Society in Philadelphia, Pennsylvania. Staying true to his reputation of being an eccentric, he has been spotted dancing in front of his statue.

President Abraham Lincoln, assassinated in April 1865, has been frequently observed wandering near the old Springfield capitol building, as well as his nearby law offices. The White House seems to be an active spirit place with First Ladies, queens, and prime ministers reportedly seeing the ghost or feeling the presence of President Lincoln.

In 2013, I was asked to participate in a paranormal investigation of historical sites in San Francisco. It's been much fun using my psychic talents while investigating the history of some of the city's interesting haunts such as the once infamous Barbary Coast and the Condor Club. At one point, as I walked through the streets, it was as though I went back in time to see men and women of an earlier era. From all I witnessed, I truly was transported to the 1800's. Never have I felt so strongly my movement through parallel dimensions of time and space. Some kind of change was felt within my physical body. I was challenged to remember I was in the present time. The exciting part, besides seeing with my psychic eye events unfold, is the historical research confirming much of my psychic visions and impressions.

My psychic findings are researched *after* the fact. I do not want my psychic impressions impaired by previous information. I have accepted, not all events or facts have a paper trail even with extensive research done by the paranormal investigators. For example, while on the streets of San Francisco's financial district, I came to an area where a massacre or intense battle of the native people occurred. After the walk, the producer's fact finding revealed the Muwekma Ohlone Indian tribes were indigenous to the Bay Area and especially along the coastline, but there is no historical record of a battle at the spot where I saw it.

The suggestions below for a ghost hunt are for the amateur ghost hunter. Investigators documenting for the advancement of paranormal studies approach ghost encounters differently. They have sensitive cameras and audio equipment and one medium or more accompanying them. No doubt they have permission to be at a location free of weekend ghost hunters. These are my experiences with ghostly encounters, and not necessarily those of other ghost investigators. Enjoy your ghost hunting but don't overly involve yourself. If you do, you might just open yourself up to troublesome, problem causing entities. Take time to rest between ghost hunts. If you would like to learn more about technical recording equipment this website is a good source: How to Conduct a Ghost Hunt www.wikihow.com/Conduct-a-Ghost-Hunt

Ghost hunting is easy. Left over energy of those who lived on earth seems to be about everywhere. Look at the obvious places, but hunt when get a *feel* of history as though you are right there in the era. This is a good start. For the more seasoned ghost hunter the following places suggested can be a fun (yes, many of we ghost hunters do consider meeting ghosts and spirits fun) although academic.

• How to begin ghost hunting: Begin where there has been reported ghost sightings. A good start for the novice ghost investigator is to tour the area where you live or are visiting to find ghost tours. Many cities and towns in most countries have them. They can be found on line or at the local tourist office. You won't have to find locations, get permission to be in the area, or worry about safety. Besides visiting a ghostly place, you'll learn a lot about local history.

If you don't take a tour, visit the library to research newspapers and books to find reported haunted buildings and locations in the area.

• Buildings and sites that might house some ghosts are listed below. Although spirits, ghosts and other entities can show up anywhere at anytime these places can be exciting to visit at nighttime.

Schools and former sites of schools: There are highly charged emotional energies, which come along with the young. The child and teenager have pure energy, and that means they are more receptive (open) to new experiences and learning. True this is how we grow in knowledge and life experiences, but with the young it also means they are more greatly open to influences beyond the physical world. Most poltergeist activity is found when younger people live or spend much of their time, like schools. The energy in schools can be felt more greatly than in say, an office building. Go to one, feel the energy both when the kids are in the hallways and even when they leave. There is a stillness, but you can feel in that stillness the voices and movement of students.

Historic buildings house the spirits of many who passed through on business. Much passed through historical buildings, people with hopes, grieves, dreams of that yet to come, fears of what would come (as in courthouses and prisons like the infamous Alcatraz). They are open to the public and may have tours. Who remembers the movie, House on the Haunted Hill (1959)? To me, it is one of the most memorable, scary movie ever! The house was a really scary place haunted by murderous ghosts and the house itself seemed to be a living, evil entity. Recently, I did a ghost investigation at The Great Star Theatre in Chinatown San Francisco where I experienced a sensation from the wood from which the theatre was built, encouraged ghost energy to thrive. I think because it's a place where many voices have been active, the vibration of them remains in the building. Consider an old theater as a possible ghostly place to hunt.

Battlefields—day or night are a great place to find ghosts because of the many, violent deaths, agony and fear that surrounds the area. There will be considerable psychic energy. A most famous haunted battleground is in a moor near Inverness, Scotland. In 1746 the English slaughtered 1,500 to 2,000 Jacobites (Highlander Clans and army supporting Charles Edward Stuart, Bonnie Prince Charlie) at the Battle of Culloden. When my husband and I were passing the area on our way to the Isle of Skye, I remarked how eerie it felt. Later, I learned the history of it. The song, "Ghost of Culloden" describes what many who passed by the moor have claimed to experienced; *Can you hear them, can you see them marching proudly across the moor. Hear the wind blow thru the drifting snow. Tell me can you see them, the ghosts of Culloden.*

Churches, opened or closed, these sacred sites are places where people celebrated every aspect of their lives with baptisms, weddings, and holy days as well as prayed for salvation. The dead in caskets are usually placed in front of the altar, and many hymns are sung. Singing raises vibration and encourages spirits into the space.

Hotels, motels or boarding houses with the many guests who stayed in these buildings and with all the dealings and goings-ons that took place in the rooms, ghost vibrations can be strong. One such boarding house I think would be a most interesting and frightening investigate is the infamous H.H. Holmes murder factory. H.H. Homes was the first serial killer in the United States who murdered quite a few unsuspecting victims in a house at 63rd and Wallace Streets in Chicago's fashionable Englewood neighbor. He lured naive young women (and a man and a few children) to board at his house. Once inside the police found a house of horrors. Rooms could be locked from the outside. A third-floor room was a veritable bank vault, padded to muffle sound and fitted with a gas pipe to asphyxiate victims. A hidden shaft to the cellar made for easy disposal of bodies. And it was the cellar of the "murder factory" where Holmes undoubtedly worked, the Tribune newspaper reported. Behind a fake wall, police found a butcher's table, quicklime vats, bones, bloody clothing — and a crematory. In the oven they found a woman's watch chain. They found the buckle of a woman's garter..." - *The Tribune*. I bet if you visit even outside the building you will feel the horror and hear the screams. That is, if you're brave enough.

Antique stores hold a wealth of psychic information! The objects for sale have a history. The ability to read history of an object is as though reading a *fingerprint* image. Fingerprints leave clues about who touched an object. Can you intuitively pick any information from an object? When you get an attraction to a particular one, hold it in your hands, close your eyes for a moment or more and truly get a *feel* from it. Along with that feel from the object you might very well sense the presence of the spirit to whom it once belonged. If it's been passed down (no doubt has been) you might pick up more than one spirit. Once you have some kind of sense of where they object came from, and/or whom it belonged to, ask the owner of the shop of any known history to confirm your impressions. In parapsychology terms the ability to feel or sense history, receive images of objects' past owners and places is called *psychometry,* and also can be referred to as *dermal vision* (seeing with the skin).

Graveyards/Cemeteries are filled with spirits and ghosts and especially eerie to visit when dark. I've read some paranormal investigative groups believe there are evil spirits in cemeteries. This could be, but I think because of the many prayers said at cemeteries there are more positive spirits than negative ones. I have yet to come across negative low-grade entities and I've been to many cemeteries, some famous for ghost sightings. If you have fearful thoughts, don't go on a ghost hunt. Remember to empty your bladder before because it may be awhile before you glimpse a spirit. Or, if you do, you may wet your pants.

• Best Time for hunting

Although, any time is good for ghostly encounters, whenever possible go on a ghost hunt when it's dark. After dark, it's quieter from the day's activities. You will catch more ghost activity between 9 p.m. to about 6 a.m. I have interacted with spirits and ghosts during the daytime.

• Proper Ghost Hunt Etiquette

Check for "Do Not Trespass" signs. Be respectful of all sites. They are the homes to spirits and ghosts whether it's because they like being where they are, or they are stuck in space and time and can't leave. Trust me, the dead don't like the living messing with their place. When I've gone to a ghost inhabited home, office, or any location, and asked them to move on, I've learned they, the spirits/ghosts, want the new occupants to move on. Therefore, negotiations must ensue.

Be polite if questioned of your intentions on the grounds. You might encounter a groundskeeper, the property owner or the police. Have one person as the spokesperson and all have identification handy if asked for it.

• Logistics.

Don't go alone. Medium or not, take a buddy. If nothing else, he or she can hold your hand if a ghost startles you or some mean person confronts you. Plus another person can help with camera and recording equipment, or to take notes and be a witness. One of you may see and hear a ghost and the other, nothing.

There is safety in numbers. Two is safer than one and up to four is good, but more than that it could get complicated with too much activity. If you are going alone, let someone know where you'll be, and when he or she can expect you back, in case of an emergency. Never place yourself in a dangerous situation.

For groups: Have everyone meet near the location to go over the plan for the ghost hunt. If you take recording equipment, decide who will work it. Choose a person or leader to talk to anyone who the group comes in contact with. (i.e. Police, Reporters, Priests, Alien Visitors, Park Rangers, etc.)

Whether you stake out a spot or you walk around, try to give everyone the opportunity to try everything and be everywhere. This keeps every one fresh and at attention. Rotate a few times during the investigation.

Take a notebook for observations on anything unusual, especially temperature changes, visual sightings and strange sounds, as well as your experiences and where, or what you want to investigate later. If the ghost is kind enough to impart words or sounds but you can't catch it on your audio recorder, you can document what was said or what sounds were heard. Others may have had the same experience when you compare notes. Also, write down any feelings or emotions you feel which may be odd or out of place.

Walk around the area to get a feel for the surroundings and allow the spirits to get a feel for you. Do this for about 20 minutes. You can also set up any stationary equipment like camera on tripods or motion detectors.

Usually, you won't encounter much at first. Keep heart though. The majority of time you will most likely encounter the spirits, especially in graveyards, of those who passed on and willingly rest in peace or the ghost who stays on earth for some reason, which you may find out. These spirits are not normally dangerous and probably won't go home with you. The spirits can be just passing through, saying their good byes to the location you are visiting or replaying their demise over and over. On a rare occasion, you may encounter an entity that was never human and this is generally bad news. I highly suggest you ignore any low life, earthbound you come across. Don't engage it in talk. Avoid it. If it bothers you, say loudly and with conviction, "QUIT IT!" or "BE GONE!"

If you have a particular protection, such as a prayer, a white light, or a lucky charm, say the prayer or chant or hold your charm close. Do not allow fear to overtake you. If you can't handle the situation, leave immediately. You can always go back once you've regrouped or you can go back with a medium.

Help set the proper atmosphere by not drinking or smoking or taking any mind-altering drugs. You don't want to imagine you saw ghosts. You want to consciously experience it, plus there is less chance of falling down in the dark and getting hurt.

Clear your mind, keep your ears open, and trust your intuition. There's no need to find ghosts or call on them to come out. They are well aware of you and watch you, observing. Maybe they are looking for the weak link, the most fearful one to spook. The person with the strongest mediumship vibration will attract the spirits and the weakest will too. Stick together.

Have a healthy skepticism. It's a better attitude for finding evidence.

Show no fear. It can attract mean-spirited entities. If you feel fear, stop, breathe, get a grip, and maybe talk about what frightens you. A ghost could have touched you or popped up at every turn. Accept it as part of the ghost hunt. If you're really frightened, leave the area and come back when you have conquered your fear enough to be rational about the ghost happenings.

Remember suggestions given in an earlier chapter about the séance conditions; before starting out on your ghost hunt, say a prayer, sing a song, a hymn, or chant. Keep a cheerful attitude and a positive frame of mind.

• Practical things to take on your ghost hunt:

Flashlights for nighttime hunting with spare batteries. Spirit activity can drain batteries very fast as well as turn off electrical lights, such as streetlights. You might bring a red lens flashlight for night vision.

Good walking shoes. Graveyards and old buildings lend themselves to uneven walks.

Warm clothing for nighttime ghost hunts which is the best time.

A face mask if you're going into an old building, which may have debris, mold or dirt. On one of my ghost hunts (Youtube Defenestration Building) we were assaulted by flocks of pigeons.

A first aid kit because you may trip in the dark or a nail could be sticking out in an old building.

Identification in case you are questioned by the police or caretaker of the property. In fact when going onto private property, you should get permission first.

Self-protection: Since you will be in a dark, spooky place take something to defend yourself, if need be, against muggers, or other living beings who might want to hurt you. It can be mace, pepper spray or even a heavy-duty flashlight.

If you have a cell phone, take it to call home or 911 if you are stuck, or otherwise need help. Make sure it is charged and check to see if it works in the area, but do turn off the ringer.

You don't want to interrupt a ghostly encounter with a ringing phone.

• Cameras and Recording Devices

Take a digital recorder to record your reactions to certain areas, and or communication with the spirit or ghost. If you're extremely lucky, you might catch an audio response of a ghost moaning, dragging chains. I doubt it though, but you might capture a whispering message. A pocket tape recorder is fine. Bring enough tape and extra batteries. Remember ghost hunters, no whispering or talking, it can taint your recording results and silence makes it easier to hear any ghosts who may make a sound.

Bring a video and photo camera and/or recording devices if you hope to catch a ghost on camera. Know how your camera and recorder works for the best results. Digital cameras can work and no need to pay the extra expenses to develop. Polaroid cameras produced fantastic results, but the cost of the film is expensive. Keep your photos, even the "bad ones" which might have flashes of streaming white lights or orbs. This is how spirit energies can appear and within the misty white substances you could very well see a figure or part of a body. Again, as suggested earlier (Chapter 1) review Dr. Hippolyte Baraduc's book, *The Human Soul: Its Movements, It's Lights and the Iconography of the Fluidic Invisible,* for photographed examples of orbs and lights surrounding a dying and dead subjects.

Check batteries and take extras. Historically there is a better chance of capturing paranormal activity in the dark. Taking photos of ghosts in well-lit environments is usually not successful. But try it anyway. Give yourself and the ghosts/spirits time to settle into the hunt by waiting about fifteen minutes before snapping photos.

Make note of streetlights and any other light source that may appear on the film. Take pictures of them for comparison purposes. When you view the developed pictures you will not think it was a ghost you shot. Watch for reflective surfaces and also take note of them. The flash reflected off shiny surfaces such as windows, polished tombstones, mirrors, eyeglasses, discarded beer bottles, etc. can look like an orb or other anomaly. If your photograph has an orb or a few of them, it can be either bugs, or dust reflection from light or the light energy of a spirit. If you feel the presence of a spirit, shoot a picture in its direction. If a light (often appears as a blurred flash) or orb shows up on your photo, you might have captured the spirit energy. Some ghost hunters say orbs are seen with the eyes, but not photographed. I think some orbs are spirit energy because I've seen too many photos with them taken by many different cameras under various conditions and time of day. Streaks of light might also appear on your photos. Some ghost hunters think of this as spirits while camera experts say it is a result of slow shutter speed. Again, you have to decide for yourself what might have happened with your camera and film. Make sure you clean your camera's lens regularly. No smoking at the location as this can appear in your photos and you might think it is a spirit whereas it was the smoke from a cigarette.

Watch for dust or dirt stirred up in the area you photograph. Both can give false positive pictures. That is unless you are shooting photos of dirt or dust. In which case record it in your notes so you don't think it was a ghost stirring it up.

Long hair should be tied back or put under a hat. Remove or tie up any camera straps so you don't take a picture of them. Again, this is to eliminate any false positive pictures and to give skeptics less ammunition.

Don't bother with your camera's viewfinder. Hold the camera out in front of you and aim at the area you want to take a picture of. Many newer digital cameras do not even come with viewfinders.

In cold weather keep the camera away from your breath so you don't photograph it. It will look like ectoplasm mist. If you think you may have caught your breath, log the picture number and discard it when you develop the pictures.

Let fellow investigators know when you are taking a photo so you don't get double flashes and the night scope operators can look away. Night scope operators can damage their eyes if they look at a flash through the scope so this is important. If you think you have a double flash photo or any other false positive, log the picture number so you can exclude the photo from the batch when they are developed.

Take pictures anywhere and everywhere. If you think you saw something, take a picture. Take photos whenever you get positive readings on any piece of equipment. If you're taking photos, snap away over the gravestones, in a corner of the room, in the garden area. You might not see a ghost with your physical eye but once the photos develop you very well may see activity not seen when taking the photo.

Sometimes you will see an orb, mist or sparkles in your flash or other's flashes. Take more pictures right there, you may be near a spirit.

• Common Ghost Sense: Tell the spirits not to follow you home and to remain where they are. Yes, this can and will happen. You don't need clingy spirits in your home.

In the next chapter, you can take my ESP (extra sensory perception) quiz to learn about your own ESP abilities and how to advance them.

■ ■ ■

12

JUNE'S ESP QUIZ

*Be careful what you think, because your thoughts run
your life.*

— Proverbs 4:23 —

Many people have had a spontaneous telepathic experience.
These experiences of thought transference or thought projection (as they also can be referred as) are often said to be a one
time or occasional experience or a coincidence. Could it be
they happen more than you think? Could it be you can learn
how to control and direct it to created rewarding experiences?
There is a shared belief between esoterical and metaphysical
studies that what you think, you become. Swiss psychiatrist and
psychotherapist, Carl Jung who founded analytical psychology,
claimed there is a synchrony between the mind and the phe-
nomenal world of perception. H. Spencer Lewis, Co-founder
and Imperator of the Rosicrucian Order, AMORC said in an

article, How Thoughts Project (Rosicrucian Digest November, 2016) "In these days, when so much is being written about the transmission of thought and its effect upon persons and conditions, it would seem that thought projection would be generally accepted as a fact and that arguments would not be necessary to prove the metaphysical laws involved."

If your thoughts can indeed create your life's experiences, how can you better understand how to direct them clearly? How will you decipher what are truly your thoughts and those from sources outside yourself? Telepathy, ESP (extra sensory perception) occurs in three ways––sending or receiving and/or both.

You may wonder why in a book about spirit communication, how does thought transference relate? It very much does relate because communication with the dead is telepathic as it is between the living. There are schools and books to teach you to develop and use your ESP positively. I can confidently recommend Litany Burn's *Your Psychic Abilities,* and for children, *The Sixth Sense of Children.* I found both helpful when teaching ESP classes. If not these book I'm sure your search for a learning source will take you to the one best for you interest.

Please understand it isn't easy to transmit clear thoughts and the effect it will have upon your target (who you're sending your message to) or conditions. Miscommunication in thought transference is mostly due to the activity of one's mind jumping from thought to thought, as well as other factors such as interference from electronic and airwaves, even certain weather conditions can interfere with clear transference. Like any other ability or talent some people will be more receptive and aware than others. This does not mean you cannot improve your telepathic skills. Receiving and sending clear messages takes practice, patience and knowledge.

My ESP/Telepathy can give you an opportunity to learn if you're a stronger receiver or sender of ESP/telepathy and how it may be occurring. The ultimate goal is to balance sending and receiving messages. Please note this test is only one of the many ways to learn about your ESP abilities. It does not necessarily determine if you have strong psychic abilities. Some very talented psychics might not score well because they often don't test well. Use it as a guide to learn about your abilities while having fun.

Choose your closet reaction and place your answer at the end of the question.

Answer with a number:

4 - always

3 - a lot

2 - sometimes

1 - rarely

0 - never

1. When the telephone rings, and before checking who is calling, or mail arrives, do you have a split second mental picture, thought, impression or feeling you know who is contacting you?

2. When the telephone rings or mail arrives, are you surprised, but not too much because for a while you had been thinking of the person?

3. Do you have strong urges or thoughts to contact someone just out of the blue, only to find (s)he had been thinking of you for a while?

4. Does it seem people respond to your wants or needs before you have a chance to ask? i.e. "I wish for a new job" and soon afterward, a friend tells you of a job?

5. Does it seem people say things you were just thinking?

6. Does it seem people say things you have been thinking about for some time?

7. Do you purposely will people to act upon your wants successfully? i.e. "I wish someone would bring me some water." and "voila!" somebody does so?

8. Do you find your wishes, dreams, or goals come true for you in life?

9. Are you a good caretaker/nurturer; giving people what they need without being asked?

10. When wanting the attention of someone without speaking or gesturing, are you successful? If you answered with 4, 3, 2, or 1 answer 10b.

<u>10b:</u> How do you get the person's attention? 1. Mentally say her/his name or a statement e.g. "Look at me!" 2. Mentally picture or imagine the person looking at you. Place your answer to 10 b in category C.

11. When you sense or think someone is looking at you, are you right? Perhaps you turn and find the person watching you or she or he confirms it later. If you answered with 4, 3, 2, or 1 answer 11b.

<u>11b:</u> How do you sense the person's attention? 1. Feel his/her eyes on the back of my head 2. Hear my name called 3. Mentally see the person's face or name 4. Have an urge to go to the person. Place your answer in category C 11b

12. Have seen or sensed non-visible movement or presence? Place your number answer in category A & C

13. Have you had vivid night or day dreams, mental pictures, images or visions and experience the same event or situation later? If you answered yes, rate your response - 4 - always • 3 - a lot • 2 - sometimes • 1- rarely and place in category C

14. Do you smell scents or odors that have no apparent source and/or others cannot? If you answered yes rate your response - • 4 - always • 3 - a lot • 2 - sometimes • 1- rarely and place in category C

15. Have you experienced a taste for no apparent reason? Meaning you have not recently, or are not eating food or drinking beverages to create that taste? If you answered yes rate your response -4 - always • 3 - a lot • 2 - sometimes • 1- rarely and place in category C

16. Do you find when around animals (all creatures) that you get a sense communication is taking place? For instance you know what the animal wants or needs e.g. water, food, to go out, medical help. If you answered yes rate your response -4 - always • 3 - a lot • 2 - sometimes • 1- rarely and place in category C

■ ■ ■

SCORE:

Category A. Place your answers:

1) ... 3) ... 5) ... 9) ... 11) ... 12) ... Total: ......

Category B. Place your answers:

2) ... 4) ... 6) ... 7) ... 8) ... 10) ... Total: ......

Category C. Place your answers below:

10b)... 11) ... 11b) ... 12b) ... 13) ... 14) ... 15) ... No total in this category

■ ■ ■

<u>Category A</u>: Receiver: A higher score in this category indicates you are a stronger receiver of messages initiated by another's or others' thought(s). For example, you think of a person moments before receiving mail or a telephone call from him/her. This is a telepathic message (a thought occurring between sources within a short period of time or instantaneous. Please note messages or knowledge about distant past or future events are a different ESP ability.) Receiving is a very rewarding communication skill to possess. You can be prepared for news and situations that will occur as well as assist others to find a "voice" when physical communication is difficult. Receivers tend to be nurturing people who like to please others by sharing their loving, helpful nature. They are often found in many healing, helping and creative arts professions. For healers, this ability is most useful to zero in on areas of the body that might not be in good health. In some way, perhaps even through thought, the healer can be helpful in the ill person healing. On the down side, a receiver/healer can become so overwhelmed with the pain she/he actually takes it on becoming ill her/himself. As an artist, the beauty of receiving inspiration from seen and unseen influences is a benefit affording you the ability to create beautiful works, which inspire others. Learn to stay aware as you open gently to energy flowing around you and endeavor to work on one creation at a time. A challenge for receivers is learning to communicate clearly their own unique and independent thoughts and needs as well and also to know what degree they are being helpful or being co-dependent.

Receivers often tend to let people be overly dependent upon them, thinking they know the answers or cure or can fix another or situation. My suggestion is to wait to be asked for help before acting. They tend to feel victimized, thinking they are being taken advantage of, or think they do too much for others and are unappreciated. There's a worrying conflict between what their thoughts and feelings are and what are those of others.

• 24 -20: You are a very keen receiver and possibly, even to some degree, a mystic, or a channeler, visionary, and/or medium. You easily communicate with unseen forces such as spirits and spirit guides and psychically see and hear beyond what most cannot. Perhaps you have been aware of these abilities even as a child. At a young age were you were aware of other dimensions and entities? Did your parents believe you? If you weren't free to express what you were experiencing, if your parents didn't understand and/or couldn't accept your visions then most likely you learned to doubt yourself or simply keep quiet about what you saw, heard and felt. That is a painful existence, is it not? In some way, at some time you understood that you have an important purpose in life, but if it wasn't encouraged or you haven't examined what your purpose might be outside the "box" of life choices, you most likely have not lived up to it—yet. Your role as a superior (or strong sender) is to bring humanity to a higher level of intelligent consciousness or enlightenment. You either are aware of this or think you must be going bonkers with grandiose ideas of saving the world. The challenge is how to find the right path to engage in your life mission. If you find yourself drawn to a needy country, one you believe you can help in some way, volunteer, seek information and support to make it a reality. If you find yourself desiring to write a book to share helpful information channeling through you, write it. You might be drawn to a religion or to one different than your own. I suggest you explore that interest. You have special gifts of love and caring, insight, healing energy and perhaps even prophecy. I suggest you find likeminded others to share your thoughts and learn how to direct your visions to a meaningful manifestation. Then again, you may be receiving too much and experience an overwhelming sense of confusion, or feel depleted, burned out to the point of exhaustion. Perhaps you are physically ill a lot. Can it be your psychic and physical and/or mental energy is so scattered from receiving an overwhelming amount of outside influences? Do you find yourself with a lot of different projects left unfinished? Have you given up finding where you fit in, if you fit in? Have you isolated yourself from interacting with others? Are you wandering from place to place? Relationship to relationship? Job to job? And feel depressed you just can't seem to find that "right" place in life? It may be you are being bombarded from receiving too much insights and information from outside of yourself that there is no focus on your own needs and goals. Truly you are lost, out of touch with your true purpose in life. Learn to take care of yourself as well as you care for others. One way is to clear your mind and body of stress and worry. Then you may harness your energy. A daily or even a periodical time for meditation can bring a wonderful sense of balance to your mind, body and spirit. Endeavor to balance serving other's needs with letting others serve you also. Accept you aren't meant to do everything, to take care of others to the point you are exhausted. Again, to successfully accomplish that stay open and accepting of a mentor, perhaps a therapist and pursue a spiritual education of your choice. Seek to understand your life purpose clearly. Ask yourself, "Why was I born?" or "What did I come to planet Earth to do?" It might be a faraway dream you once had, even as a child. It can feel so right when you recall that special dream. You know it is exactly the right thing to do. Once you have calmed your life problems, are refreshed and reclaimed your power you will be clear with a worthwhile purpose.

• 19-14: You have a big heart and want to be helpful. You are clearly receiving information, but might be confused to the validity of it. Strengthen your confidence. Playing telepathic games with another is one way. Another way is to validate your messages e.g. ask the person you are thinking of, if the message received is in line with her/his thoughts or situation. Become clearer with messages through understanding how you receive them. It can be as symbols, dreams, visions, hearing words and/or receiving images or pictures. See more below in category C. Define your mission. What are you meant to do in life? Are you interested in the healing world? Perhaps you've thought about studying to be a doctor, nurse, psychotherapist, coach, or health trainer. Maybe you already are one of those. Choosing a professional role can certainly add a sense of worthwhile meaning to your receiving abilities. What you clearly must do is learn to draw boundaries, then you will save energy for your goals. In your personal life, you will learn how to serve others in kindness, but not take on total responsibly for what others can do for themselves. To refresh your psychic and mental energy spend time in nature. Think about taking up an artistic pursuit for the pure joy of creating for that alone will balance your enjoyment for fulfilling self-interest with what you give to others.

• 13-7: Two situations may be occurring. It can be you receive too much information and have mentally shut down. That means you walk around in a fog or your goals and responsibilities are half done, not fulfilling and you are exhausted more often than refreshed. Then again you might be too busy sending mental thoughts to build and create that you've become unaware of anything but your needs. Most likely you are a natural at receiving information but somewhere along the course of life you "burned out" giving and doing for others that you went to the extreme—all about you. To balance receiving and not shutting down emotionally, you can learn to enjoy giving. Once you have set boundaries do for others what you reasonably can and feel good about doing. Pay attention to what and who surrounds you and how it emotionally, physically and mentally affects you. Learn to listen to others verbally and non-verbally without jumping in to be the savior or helper. Also, don't go the other way, which is not helping anyone at all. Your relationships may improve as you learn to balance and stick to healthy boundaries. Validate the messages you receive by, if possible, asking if the person was thinking or needing whatever you picked up. Develop a schedule that includes a time to sit quietly to relax your mind and body. You are free to choose. Journaling may also be helpful to set your mind free of the many things you are receiving. Life is good when you learn to balance it.

• 6-1: Somewhere along the course of life you have lost focus on your true self and what your life purpose is. This might be because you are spending too much time on your own thing, goals and/or problems. Have others said it seems you must always be in control? Do you work too hard for what you want and are unavailable for relationships, health care or anything outside your interest? In other words, are you so obsessed with projects, or worries that there is no place for anyone or anything in life? Then again, you can be like a rag doll controlled by serving others' needs so much that you feel victimized and think life is just not fair; "When is it my turn?" Does your life feel out of control, scattered? You may be missing messages, signs giving you the "go-ahead" with your goals and dreams. Now is time to realize, you count too! It's time for you to learn how to take care of yourself in healthy, rewarding ways. Read about co-dependents, creative visualization and manifestation. It can also be you are a very strong receiver but somewhere along the course of life have turned away from your ESP impressions. Perhaps you turned away because of fear—someone in the past telling you it's false messages, or against God's teaching or will, or you have been made fun of when sharing your feelings and thoughts. Maybe you are afraid of what you envision or dream thinking if something bad happens it's your fault for knowing before-hand. It would serve you for the best to get guidance from a mentor, someone who understands how ESP works. Or, read a book on the subject and experiment with it. Take time to think about your score. After a period of time, retake the test.

■ ■ ■

<u>Category B Sender:</u> A higher score here indicates you are a strong sender of telepathic messages. You have the ability to create what and who you need to assist you in accomplishing your mission and goals. Senders are more often the action type people, confident leaders that move forward with determined purpose. Senders can accomplish goals easily when they have clarity of purpose and are relaxed in their role of creating for the better of humanity. They can be quite articulate in speech, good planners and great visionaries. Trained properly, they can be powerful healers by sending energy through another's body and even into the world. Highly developed senders contribute to the spiritual growth of the world by sending powerful messages that advances humanity to higher levels of intellect and spiritualism. Spiritually advanced senders know how to take and give fairly, balancing their goals so all realize fulfillment. Senders attract willing participants easily to help them achieve goals. But they can, and will, control, manipulate and dominate to get what they want, no matter what the cost. A sender may be so focused on their goals they are or become tunnel-visioned, not paying attention to the often-subtle responses of attainment. They are often perfectionist, demanding much of themselves and others. Because they are mentally busy, they are highly agitated, overly aggressive, stressful and often, volatile.

Senders have a wonderful ability to vision and create usually, with ease. They are focused to attain success and fulfillment in a way most wish for. When senders are in balance of sending and receiving (without their ego getting swollen out of proportion) they bring positive and progressive changes.

There are many ways to develop and use your sending abilities such as writing a goal or need, seeing it clearly in a simple form, and then sending the image telepathically. When clear of purpose and intention, a quick response to the message will occur.

• 24- 20: You are a highly developed sender, connected to a Higher Source, consciously or not. That source is sending you what and who is needed to create and to manifest a happy successful life on your karmic path. You are a leader, an innovator and highly respected for what you can contribute to the world. Let's face it, you have charisma! No doubt people want to be with you, listen to your sage advice, and take part in your visions. Recognize the helpful loving people who are supporting your goals. On the other side of strong senders is how they can use their will to be self-serving. Be aware of how you might dominate, control and/or manipulate others to submit to your way. Trust the process if you find confusion arises over how to attain with willing partners. Be more patient. When manifesting a goal you can be obsessed and overly focused, losing a sense of balance of your goals with those goals and needs of others. You do have the power to positively affect people and even the world. No doubt, you have a wonderfully charming ability to create a win-win situation. Remember to share your rewards. Review if you are balanced between sending (taking) and receiving (giving).

• 19-14: You are aware of what you want, and usually you get it, but with effort. As the Rolling Stones' song says, "You can't always get what you want, but if you try sometimes you get what you need." Learn to listen on a physical and non-physical level to more easily receive spoken or unspoken messages. They can be subtle like for instance you want to travel. Everywhere you are, waiting for public transportation you see billboards with travel ads appearing in front of your eyes. Or, something you seek an answer is to is addressed by at least three people within a short period of time, each telling you the same thing. Pay heed. Stay aware of what goes on around you and you might see or hear go-ahead messages confirming what you asked for. This way you know what you plan, hope for and are working toward is in the process of manifesting. Also, keep an open ear and mind to other's viewpoints. Don't look for the perfect result. Take a more patient approach; a step-by-step process to where you are going. Review your progress every so often (don't always skip ahead into the future) to see if you are in the flow or pushing too hard. Learn to keep your thoughts clear and simple to more easily manifest your vision. Life doesn't have to be an uphill struggle. You have strong abilities to attract most of what you wish for in life. Take time to refine those abilities through meditation to free the many thoughts in the mind so you are completely clear what you are attracting to you and why.

• 13-7: Perhaps you are not as direct as you can be with what you want from life. You might be mentally scattered with too much on your mind. Learn to clear your mind and be more focused on what you wish to accomplish. You might be taking care of others by being overly involved in their lives. Most likely believing you are doing what is best for them. Do you give unasked for advice (even if you are asked try to refrain from comment)? Or, give something to make their lives better without being asked to do so? Stop! Focus on your own self. Do you have specific goals? If so, what are they? What is your plan, your target date to fulfill those goals? Or, do you just take life as it comes? No plan, no expectations, no direction? You may not be aware that what you receive in life is really what you think you should have. If it seems no one cares for you, then most likely most don't even acknowledge you. If you believe that life is hard and trying, then unhappy events and people will surround you and drag you down to support that belief. If you don't like what life is offering you, check your thoughts for depressing, fearful or doubtful ones. Practice stating your wish or goal and ending with "I know this or something better will come into my life." Count your blessings daily for the simple and good things in your life like your vision, hearing, walking, food, a place to lay your head etc.

• 6-1: Who is running and over influencing your life? Do you think life is just by chance or dominated by fate or others? Do you often experience feeling empty or victimized by circumstances? It could be at one time, maybe as a young person, you were more assertive in achieving goals and for some reason have closed off to those once important goals? Perhaps you weren't supported or belittled and now feel defeated and, most likely, depressed. Most likely you give too much of your time and energy. I highly suggest you find a psychotherapist, a psychologist, or a family therapist to discuss your feelings and heal your wounds. Learn to be more conscious of how *you* play a part in creating life experiences and relationships by what you mentally envision and expect. Be alert who supports you feeling down and used and/or "no good". Become aware how this is happening. Is it the words they use? Do they say negative, harmful things about you or about life? It might be a close relationship or a group of people. It can be the media, even your choice of entertainment (television programs, movies, music). This all has an impact on your psyche. Even how you talk is powerful in creating what your experiences. If you make negative statements about life those words carry a message, an energy that will match your statement. Read 13-7 outcome above for more about your options. Decide you will speak more positively about yourself and life. Find positive affirmations to write and say aloud. See Louise Hay's affirmations. I use them regularly. They have changed my life for the best! Life has many joyful rewards!

■ ■ ■

<u>Category C:</u>
• 10b: #1 clairaudio (clear sound). Hearing and/or speaking words or statements, and/or sounds psychically not physically occurring. Sending words mentally or aloud telepathically when receiving or sending to attract what you want. For the best results learn to focus on speaking clear simple words. Use one or two strong word(s) to support what you are manifesting. If receiving, calm your mind and search for "key" words to have a clear message. #2 clairvoyant (clear sight). Mentally or psychically seeing messages such as an image, symbol, picture or even on-going action, like watching a film. To receive a clear message, again, calm your mind and watch the message emerge. To send a clairvoyant message be focused and keep it simple i.e. one image at a time, not jumping around. If too many come at one time, breathe and accept only one.

• 11b: #1 and/or #4: clairsentience (clear sense) can also be known as sensitives or empathics. This is associated with having a "gut feeling" although you might feel a tingle, tightening or any physical sensation in another place in your body. The reference to gut feeling corresponds to the second chakra located around the belly button, and it associated with deep emotional feeling. Picking up the feelings, thoughts and energy of others. This can be the most difficult ESP ability to translate into a verbal message. To begin to verbalize your feelings see an image or a series of them symbolizing your feeling or even a color of those feelings. Settle yourself into a calm state and then practice running your feeling (which usually start in the gut, but can come from anywhere in your body) upward like a stream of energy to the middle of your forehead (the middle eye or vision center). Once you have a clearer idea of what you wish to communicate, do so and trust you will be understood. The same applies before sending a message or receiving one, take your time to put your feelings into an image, color and/or words.

If your answer is number #2 you are a clairaudient. You psychically/mentally (not with the physical use of sound) hear words or sounds. It can be if someone is talking to you or it is your voice talking to yourself. Messages need not come in the form of words. It might be a sound surrounding you or from another time. Like a train roaring past although no train is around you. That train might symbolize travel to you. Later another talks about plans to travel, or you decide to go on a trip. You might hear a door opening whereas there is no sound near you indicating a door has moved. It is then you realize a spirit has entered your atmosphere. To clearly receive messages, calm your mind so thoughts are not overflowing with many messages. Then you have a better chance of receiving the telepathic/ESP message. Take note of what you think have heard. It can be useful at a later date. Automatic writing is associated with clairaudio. That is an ESP ability to be in a trance like state and write messages received while in that frame of mind.

If you answered with #3 you are a clairvoyant. This is the ESP ability to psychically see (not with the physical eyes) images, objects, people, faces, colors, and/or symbolism connected to a psychic occurrence. It can be an image from the past (recognition), the present or the future (precognition). If in the present time, it is clearly telepathy. Whatever you see doesn't exist in a physical form at the time you are having the vision. If it is the past and you have no prior knowledge of it, it is recognition. You might give details of a person, a building or an area from another era and upon investigating, find you saw clearly. If precognition, knowing or seeing the future perhaps you see a person you don't know. The person might be one you meet at a later time: same as with a location or event. Most people who experience ESP are prone to clairvoyance. That might be because we already experience most of what happens as in mental picture form.

• 12. Your number answer will help determine your level of ESP. Feeling the presence of non-visible energy indicates you have, to some degree, the ability to communicate with non-physical entities be that spirits, ghosts, angelic beings etc. Learn to relax when in contact to see and feel the presence as in an image form. Say "Hello" or "Welcome" mentally or aloud. Doing so will help you make a connection. You might hear back a greeting. Or, if you feel threatened or uncomfortable with the entity say firmly, "That's enough, leave me alone!" and/or "Leave!" Do not agree to "house" the entity or spirit, as in come through me. Keep your control by be willing to see, as though at a distance the message that is being sent.

• 13. Dreams nighttime or daytime or visions that manifest into real life experiences indicate that you have moved beyond telepathy into precognition—knowing the future or having a premonition. This can be thought of as claircognizance - being clearly cognizant (aware or mindful) of that which is yet to occur. Knowing of an event without having prior knowledge. Life shouldn't be too surprising when you see where you're going. Learn to use it wisely.

• 14 and 15. The sensation of smelling or tasting that, which does not physically exist in your immediate surroundings, is called clairgustance. You are receiving a psychic message through the sense of taste and/or smell without it be remnants of something you recently ate, or is in your presence (seeing foods can generate a sense of taste as in saying "my mouth watered") or smelling something in your physical vicinity or even been nearby. An example, you might experience a taste or smell of spicy foods and later be invited to join in a dinner serving them.

• 16. If you answered yes in this category you accept communication occurs between humans and animals. Most animal lovers know when their pet need or want something––pet e.g. I want out, pick me up, feed me, let's play, etc. Often times other needs, i.e. I'm ill, I feel lonely, frightened etc. can become more difficult to decipher why and what is best to do for the animal.

One of the biggest challenge humans have with animal communication is translating the animal's mode of communication into human understanding and back to the animal. Most animal communication is through body language (i.e. growl, purr, whine, bark, meow, whinny). To deepen your connection to the animal of your interest learn about its body language. An easy example is majority of animals take staring directly at them as threatening. I hear people talk on and on to animals, using multiple words. In return the animal looks at the human with a *"what are you taking about?"* expression or just ignores the words (unless it contains a treat word). Remember, communication is a two-way conversation. When you catch the attention of the animal, more communication will open.

I've communicated with my own pets and those of others with astonishing results. I have learned not all animals will communicate with me, not all animals are clear with their needs, not all animals listen well (put humans on ignore), and a ready response doesn't or doesn't appear to the human to take place at the time.

Animal communication is in images, pictures and/or a series of them and can include smells. Animals rely much on scents and odors to survive. Here is an example of a horse communicating with me through smell. A woman called to ask for my help to understand why her horse was so depressed. She understood because he was in a different living situation it would take time, but it had been a couple of months since the move. The horse was in a large pasture with other horses. He stood alone. I introduced myself to him, let him sniff me and then touched his neck (making contact). He seemed to enjoy our connection as I continued to stroke him. My first intuitive sense was the smell of burning wood (clairgustance ability). I breathed it in and opened my senses to receive more information. In my mind's eye an image of smoke spiraling from a chimney set atop a small cabin emerged. In my mind's eye I saw the horse grazing near the cabin. I related the scene to the horse owner who confirmed before she had the horse he had lived as an only horse on a small acreage near a house where there had been a wood burning stove as I described. I further related to the woman the horse's emotional memory: he missed the scent as it provided a sense of security for him. He and his former person got along very well he told me. Again, the woman confirmed the former owner was elderly who, for health reasons, had to re-home the horse. He now lived in a large field with other horses. He said he felt insecure in the herd. His standing away from the other horses confirmed that easily. I spied a smaller paddock adjacent the field and asked if he could be moved there. At that moment the horse turned back to me (I was standing at his shoulder) and nosed my hand. I took it as an affirmation that's what the horse needed. I made another request; would the woman please burn some wood or a sage stick for the horse? She agreed and also moved him into the paddock. In time the horse perked up and made horse friends over the fence. The owner considered moving him back with the herd.

You will learn the way to communicate that best suits your abilities. After studying the animal's body language here are some suggestions to begin your telepathic communication: begin by calming your mind and body (being at ease), send a love feeling from your heart to the animal then talk softly and quietly (animals' hearing is sharp) with a few simple words (hello, hi I'm ___). You might want to hum or sing quietly. If the animal is willing and when safe to do so, get close and ask, "Can I touch you?" The animal will let you know no doubt through body language.

If your ability is clairvoyance––that's a big plus as you already receive information through image form. If you are a clairaudient translate words into images––the words paint a picture. Send the image back to the animal. This tells the animal he or she is being heard. The animal might send information about past history, present condition, or relate a funny story (many animals have a wonderful sense of humor). If the animal is frightened, angry or confused console it.

Clairsentients, sensitives and empathics will do well since animals' feelings guide them. Your challenge is to allow those feelings to translate into images relating to the actual animal's experience and not become the emotion. It could be emotionally intense and draining especially if dealing with an abused or unhappy animal.

It's not easy to have clear communication with animals at all times. In grave situations it can be even more difficult because of urgent needs. This might be when you wish to find an animal communicator.

There are many good books on this topic. Some examples are Carol Gurney's "The Language of Animals: 7 Steps to Communicating with Animals" and Margrit Coates' "Communicating with Animals: How to Tune into Them Intuitively." You might enjoy watching on Youtube.com animal communicator, Anna Breytenbach's incredible story about Diabolo, a leopard, who became known as Spirit.

■ ■ ■

Remember, the purpose of understanding your personal ESP abilities is to seek a balance between receiving and sending—give and take—in order harmony and joy is created within and without. You can open up each of your *clair-senses* (corresponds with the five physical senses) through first having an understanding how they work and by experimenting. I see, I hear, I feel or sense, I taste, I smell, I experience. As you utilize your ESP you create a full experience of the seen and unseen worlds.

Do not be afraid to "be wrong" because chances are you are not entirely incorrect. Time will tell, and if it doesn't, your ESP is still setting you on a path to experience more of life's opportunities. Follow through and learn as you go. In time you will be more comfortable with your ESP. Understand and trusting your ESP––your psychic intuitive messages––will aid you in making life choices and decisions proper for your spiritual advancement. As you confidently make choices based upon your clear senses to what is right and meaningful you, your talents, you live with a clear purpose and life will be most fulfilling.

Please note: If you experience any of the above and think or sense or another thinks it is a medical condition––physical or psychological––please seek advice from your health care practitioner.

■ ■ ■

BIBLIOGRAPHY

Ahern, June, *The Timeless Counselor: The Best Guide to a Successful Psychic Reading*, November 11, 2013

Albom, Mitch, *The Five People You Meet In Heaven*, March 1, 2006

Alexander III, Eden, Dr., *Proof of Heaven: A Neurosurgeon's Journey into the Afterlife*, October 23, 2012

Article: *Ain't no Way Go* Jimmy "The Bear" Ferrozzo www.aintnowaytogo.com/pianoSex.htm

Baraduc, Hippolyte Dr., *The Human Soul: Its Movements, It's Lights and the Iconography of the Fluidic Invisible*, Published before 1923. Revised August 19, 2011

Blatty, Peter, *The Exorcist*, 1971

Budapest, Z. (Zsuzanna), *The Grandmother of Time*, October 18, 1989

Burns, Litany, Develop *Your Psychic Abilities*, December 1, 1988

Burns, Litany, *The Sixth Sense of Children*, February 1, 2002

Coates, Margrit, *Communicating with Animals: How to Tune into Them Intuitively*, May 3, 2012

Conroy-Costello, Rebecca, RN, Suffering During the Dying Process Has a Purpose, Fate Magazine, Issue No. 729, 2015

Doyle, Arthur Conan, *The New Revelation,* January 1, 1918

Gurney, Carol, *The Language of Animals: 7 Steps to Communicating with Animals,* August 7, 2001

Hay, Louise, *You Can Heal Your Life,* January 1, 1984

Huxely, Aldous, *Devils of Loudun,* 1959 & July 28, 2009

Kübler-Ross, Elisabeth, M.D. *On Death and Dying,* July 2, 1997

Lee, Carroll and Tober, Jan, *The Indigo Children: The New Kids Have Arrived,* May 1, 1999

Losey, Meg, PhD, *The Children of Now: Crystalline Children, Indigo Children, Star Kids, Angels on Earth, and the Phenomenon of Transitional Children,* December 1, 2006

MacGregor, Rob, Necromanteion: Oracle of the Dead in Greece: Sailing up the mysterious Acheron River to the Greek Underworld of Hades - On-line article

Melies, George, (first horror film) "Le Manoir du Diable", released Winter 1896 - 1897

Mitchell, Karyn, *Walk-Ins/Soul Exchange,* October 1, 1999

Montgomery, Ruth, *Strangers Among Us,* November 12, 1984

Moody, Raymond Jr. M.D. 1975 *Life After Life,* 1975 & September 8, 2015

Moody, Raymond Jr., M.D. with Perry, Paul, *Reunions: Visionary Encounters with Departed Loved Ones,* October, 31, 1994

Moorjani, Anita, *Dying To Be Me: My Journey From Cancer to Near Death, To True Healing,* December 17 2011 - September 1, 2014.

Perry, Yvonne, *Walk-ins Among Us,* May 1, 2013

Rosicrucian Digest, Volume 94, Number 2, 2016

Smith, Penelope, *Animals in Spirit,* January 8, 2008

Stengar, Victor, "Life After Death: Examining the Evidence" - The Huffington Post article April 15, 2012

Taylor, Bolte, Jill, *My Stroke of Insight: A Brain Scientist's Personal Journey*, May 12, 2008

Time-Life, *Mysteries of the Unknown, Psychic Voyages*, 1987-1991

US News & World Report, March 1997

White, Blunt, Mary, *Letters From the Other Side: With Love, Harry and Helen*, January. 1988

Willin, Melvyn, M.D., *Ghosts Caught on Film: Photographs of the Paranormal and The Paranormal Caught on Film 1 and 2*, September 23, 2008

■ ■ ■

Thank you for reading my book. I hope what I shared about communicating with the dead and finding ghosts has helped you to determine if it is possible to be in contact with them. Are you ready for the adventure?

Would you please leave a review at your favorite book retailer's website? *June Ahern*, Author

■ ■ ■

ACKNOWLEDGEMENTS

Thank you to all who made this book possible: my editor, Deidre Murphy for supporting me to the end result; Chad Ramirez, you insisted I write this book, although I told you 'no' enough times before acquiescing. You were right, I did have to share my stories and spirit experiences; it's been quite a journey back into ghostly adventures. To my Red Pen ladies: Mary, Marianna, and Sherry and Red Penciled gentleman, Jerry, my husband for your continual kindness through my ups and downs of writing. Ying Liu, Producer of The Haunted Bay: SF and Beyond, and her film/sound crew, Cody Kulka and filmmaker, Matthew Abaya for some great paranormal investigations. To my son, Daniel, who has been a creative inspiration from day one of his life. If I have forgotten anyone, please know I am thankful for your help.

■ ■ ■

ABOUT JUNE AHERN

June is an author of four books, numerous articles, and two screenplays. She has had a successful career as a psychic/medium since 1975. Although, retired her private practice in 2014 she continues sharing her talents on ghost investigations with The Haunted Bay and Beyond. Presently, she continues with her Life Coaching practice, is finishing the sequel to *The Skye in June*, lecturing, and traveling for book events. She lives in Northern California on the coast.

Archives of her radio talk show can be heard at readingsbyyerevan.com. On the website, click Radio Shows upper right hand, scroll to Authors & Spiritual Teachers, and then to June Ahern.

CONTACT JUNE AHERN

For latest books updates and scheduled events review at www.juneahern.com. June's coaching practice can be reviewed at www.sfcoaching.com.

The Haunted Bay paranormal ghost investigation videos at Youtube.com/thehauntedbay

Facebook.com/juneahernbooks

Favorite Amazon.com or Smashwords author page: www.smashwords.com/profile/view/JuneA

■ ■ ■

INTRODUCTION TO JUNE AHERN'S
OTHER BOOKS

■ ■ ■

THE TIMELESS COUNSELOR:
The Best Guide to a Successful Psychic Reading

■ ■ ■

Do not believe in a thing because many have said it.
After examination, believe that which you have tested
for yourselves and found reasonable, which is in confor-
mity with your well-being and that of others.

— *Buddha* —

My psychic reader said... Ears perk up when a statement of this kind is made. It certainly invites discussion - pro or con.

Have you ever considered having a psychic reading? If so, do you wonder how you would you find a trustworthy psychic? Can a reading be a good source for helping you make wise decisions and set valuable goals? These questions and more will be answered in *The Timeless Counselor: The Best Guide to a Successful Psychic Reading.* It is your complete guide to receiving the greatest benefits from a psychic reading. In it you will learn how to choose a reader personally suitable for your interest, how to prepare for your session, ask questions to get the most information from the reader, and afterwards, how to use the information favorably.

I am not trying to convert you to believe in a subject you might be opposed to but rather to share my, over forty years, experiences as a psychic reader and metaphysical teacher and

to dispel the mysteries, superstitions and misconceptions surrounding psychic readers and readings.

■ ■ ■

*This book is a complete consumer's guide to receiving the most from a
psychic reading.* Suzette Martinez Standring, author of *The Art of
Column Writing*

■ ■ ■

THE SKYE IN JUNE

Chapter One
Glasgow, Scotland
May 31, 1950

The rain drizzling down the windows of the taxi shrouded the riders inside. Cathy MacDonald, the sole passenger, leaned her head against the misted window. She was bound for St. Andrew's Infirmary to deliver yet another wean.

The taxi driver startled her, and she wondered if he had heard her question. "I know all about how fast those weans want out. Got six bairns of my own," he said, laughing loudly.

Cathy didn't dare tell him that her labor pains were coming very close together and that this might be the first time that a baby would be born in his taxi.

"Your man's Jimmy MacDonald, right?" he inquired.

His talking only irritated her but not wanting to appear unfriendly she tried to focus on what he had asked. Her response came as a muffled sound that could have been an answer or a retreat from the question. She caught him peeking a glance at her in the rearview mirror. She braced herself for the next question, knowing what it would be.

"You Mr. B's daughter?"

The driver, along with so many others in Glasgow, deeply respected Willie Buchanan, or Mr. B, as he had been known for as far back as anyone could remember. Mr. B had earned a reputation for being a fair man. Years ago he had rallied a group of well-off citizens to provide funds to support youth soccer teams for the towns underprivileged children. He had insisted that the money be shared equally between Catholic and Protestant teams––an unusual act, since prejudice between the two religious groups was still very intense in Scotland. Although some people protested, most citizens supported his efforts.

The taxi swerved sharply to avoid a pile of building rubble. Cathy moaned in protest, which made the driver wish her husband was there to help with the situation. "Where's Jimmy?" he asked.

Chapter 1
Chowchilla, California
Chowchilla State Women's Facility
1984

Snap, snap, snap. The rapid sharp sounds of the inmate's bubblegum ricocheted around the waiting room.

"Brenda Rose!" growled Officer Sue DeLosa between clenched teeth, followed by a threatening glare. Brenda Rose Browne, or BR as she was known at Chowchilla's Women's Correctional Facility, scowled defiantly at the stout officer and continued rotating her jaw like a cow chewing cud. DeLosa widened her stance and casually placed a hand next to her truncheon. The prisoner rolled her watery blue eyes at her fellow inmate, Liz Mackay, sitting opposite on a matching plastic chair.

Liz ignored both women and fixed her eyes straight ahead on the blank wall. The gum chomping and snapping didn't irritate her as it did the guard. She'd learned to live with many irritants and restrictions over the years she'd been incarcerated.

What did annoy Liz was the escalating stale odor emanating from the women's bodies in the cramped windowless room. The space was more of a wide corridor with three doors. At one end a door led to the cellblocks and eight feet away opposite it another led to offices and the outside. Behind the third door in the middle was where the parole board conducted hearings to determine prisoners' lives. The three women had been waiting for almost an hour while the board settled in and reviewed their cases.

Liz tilted her head back to rest against the wall and tried to calm her growing anxiety. She wondered why she agreed to face the parole board again. No matter which board she faced, it would be the same: parole denied. Anger at her attorney, Toni Bordeaux, also nagged at her. The previous day they had had a serious argument. The words played over and over in her mind and Liz began to doubt her decision.

■ ■ ■

Liz studied the woman she'd had known for seventeen years. Toni's shiny, black hair was now peppered with grey and cut close to her skull. Her dark brown face looked nearly as youthful as when Liz first saw her. Toni was wearing her usual dark, tailored pantsuit, and simple, yet expensive jewelry. On her lap was an opened briefcase that held a large file full of papers associated with Liz's case. "When did your penance turn into self-punishment?" demanded Toni.

■ ■ ■

I was hooked on page one. one of those books that are hard to put down. It's a classic San Francisco tale.

—Sal Valdez, Amazon Reviewer

It's easy for people to romanticize the Summer of Love, but Ms. Ahern portrays the underlying grit very well. Great end twist with the parole hearing visitor!

—Tammy A, Amazon Reviewer

■ ■ ■

More reviews:
juneahern.com
Amazon.com
Smashwords.com
Barnes and Nobels.com

63490039R00130

Made in the USA
Lexington, KY
08 May 2017